"Readers of Nancy Brummett's newest book, *Take My Hand Again*, will find themselves in the pages of real-life stories about families and their journeys through aging. They will be comforted in discovering that they are not alone in their mixed-up feelings. Nancy has written a practical yet hope-filled book that is sure to help both younger and older generations reexamine their roles with love and grace as together they navigate through the uncertainties of later years."

—Missy Buchanan, speaker and author of *Voices of Aging:*
Adult Children and Aging Parents Talk with God

"Nancy Parker Brummett takes readers by the hand to walk with them through key issues involved in caring for aging parents, using her Christian faith to narrate the meanings of the journey. Her warm, tender approach is grounded in both personal experience and careful research. Very human stories richly illustrate aging dilemmas, resilience, loss, gains, poignant moments, grace, and a sense of purpose. Information and resources offer guidance for those feeling alone and lost in the process as well as those preparing for the future. The book could be a personal guide or a group study experience for midlife adults, all with a focus on maximizing the respect and dignity of older adults while comforting those providing care."

—Sara Honn Qualls, clinical geropsychologist and
author of *Caregiver Family Therapy*

"This is the most comprehensive book on aging and caregiving I've ever seen. It is an excellent resource for anyone facing either one or both of these issues. Great stories, great ideas, great solutions!"

—Dr. Helen B. McIntosh, counselor and author of
Messages to Myself: Overcoming a Distorted Self-Image

"A thoughtful and loving guide to what can be an emotionally fraught period of time when adult children take on the role of caregiver to their aging parents. Easy to read and full of examples and stories of how families can approach this time. We know that they will face significant life changes such as managing chronic illness or moves to assisted-living facilities. I hope that readers of this book are filled not only with information but also with hope as they lead their parents into the future."

—Beth Hall Roalstad, MSW, executive director of Innovations in Aging Collaborative

"Nancy's words flow from deep devotion to the aging community and those who care for them. *Take My Hand Again* is replete with endearing anecdotes of caring for precious parents and is filled, from cover to cover, with detailed and practical paths to accomplish that care. I was deeply moved throughout—tears, laughter, and resolve jockeyed for equal attention. This invaluable book will certainly find its way into the hands of my children, so that they won't miss a beat in my end-of-life care!"

—Alice Scott-Ferguson, speaker, writer, and author of *Mothers Can't Be Everywhere But God Is*, and *Reconcilable Differences* coauthored with Nancy Parker Brummett

"I love this encouraging and helpful book, *Take My Hand Again*. As a young couple my wife and I took in her mother to live with us. I wish we'd had a copy of this book then."

—Pastor Ron Ritchie, author of *Free at Last!*

"This book reminds us that many times along our life-walk, the path becomes obscure. We need someone to help show us the way and that someone is God. I am reminded of Proverbs 16:3—'Commit to the Lord whatever you do, and your plans will succeed.' This book will certainly help adult children who now find themselves in a role reversal situation."

—Ken & Sylvia Ringling, owners of Interim HealthCare, Colorado Springs, Colorado

TAKE
MY
HAND
AGAIN

Also by Nancy Parker Brummett

The Hope of Glory
It Takes a Home
The Journey of Elisa
Reconcilable Differences
Simply the Savior

TAKE MY HAND AGAIN

A FAITH-BASED GUIDE
FOR HELPING **AGING PARENTS**

NANCY PARKER BRUMMETT

Kregel
Publications

Take My Hand Again: A Faith-Based Guide for Helping Aging Parents
© 2015 by Nancy Parker Brummett

Published by Kregel Publications, a division of Kregel, Inc., 2450 Oak Industrial Dr. NE, Grand Rapids, MI 49505.

The persons and events portrayed in this book have been used with permission. To protect the privacy of these individuals, names and identifying details may have been changed.

Scripture quotations are from the Holy Bible, New International Version®, NIV®. Copyright © 1973, 1978, 1984 by Biblica, Inc.™ Used by permission of Zondervan. All rights reserved worldwide. www.zondervan.com

ISBN 978-0-8254-4371-8

Printed in the United States of America

15 16 17 18 19 / 5 4 3 2 1

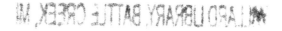

*To all who pray, hope, and care for the
aging parents they love*

Contents

Acknowledgments

I'm grateful to both my mother and mother-in-law for modeling courageous and graceful aging to me. Thank you, Lois Whitehead Parker and Mary Frances Brummett, for giving me so many stories to tell and memories to share. I miss you both so very much.

I'm also indebted to my sisters, Patty Watkins and Mary Slack, superb caregivers both, and to the many friends who also opened their hearts to share their journeys in caring for their aging parents. We cried and laughed together over the years, and we helped one another survive.

The University of Colorado at Colorado Springs (UCCS) Gerontology Department fed my hunger for more academic information through their Professional Advancement Certificate in Gerontology program. I'm grateful for the knowledge gleaned from the lecturers and classmates in that excellent course of study.

I'm also forever grateful to my husband, Jim Brummett. I'm so glad we were able to help one another care for our moms and so hopeful we will be able to grow old together and give our adult children the opportunities for growth through caregiving that our moms gave us. That's how it works, isn't it?

Finally and always, to God be the glory! It is He who urges, inspires, and ultimately creates anything that is created, including this book.

Introduction

The ringing phone jars you awake in the middle of the night. You manage to get it to your ear and the voice on the other end tells you your mother fell and is being taken to the emergency room. Or you leave a visit with your dad, and as soon as you get in the car, you put your head down and just let the tears flow. You know you can't ignore the signs any longer. He's not doing well in his present living situation. His basic safety is at risk.

Regardless of how the realization dawns on us that our elderly parents need us to intervene in their care, we are seldom ready. Most of us with aging parents prefer the comfort of denial—that they will go on as they are indefinitely. Their lives will stay the same and so will ours. They'll continue to make their own decisions about housing, doctors, medications, and diet, and we'll continue to meet the demands of our busy lives with only the occasional visit and phone call to stay in touch.

But as those who have traveled down this road know full well, change is inevitable. Ready or not, circumstances shift, and so do the familiar family roles developed over a lifetime. Overnight, you realize that your role is now more that of parent than son or daughter, and the elder you love—the one you've depended on for guidance and help all your life—is now turning to you for support.

The many questions this transition entails can keep you awake at night. How much involvement is necessary or wanted? How will the elders you love respond to your well-intentioned efforts to help? And while roles change, isn't it disrespectful to say that we are parenting our parents? After all, they will always be a generation ahead of us. And we will always be their kids.

Beginning the journey of caring for your aging parent can feel like being dropped off in a foreign country where you don't know the language and don't even have a reliable map or GPS. Fortunately, others have traveled this road ahead of you and are willing to share what they've learned to make your journey go more smoothly.

Take My Hand Again is a starting place for those headed down this long, winding path of caregiving. If you are reading this book, chances are you've already gotten the wake-up call that life as you know it is about to change. Or you are wise enough to know that being in denial about your parent's aging won't help either of you navigate this next stage of life together. You want to be prepared for what's to come: to anticipate the signs that change is necessary and to know the questions to ask and the potholes to avoid.

Those who discover they must now intervene and care for an elder they love often desperately wish they had a wise and experienced friend—someone who has traversed this path ahead of them and can direct the journey. It's my prayer that by sharing useful, encouraging information mixed with hope, humor, and faith, *Take My Hand Again* will be that trusted companion for you.

God placed us in families for a reason. While your aging parent's situation and your role in your family may be changing dramatically, none of these changes takes God by surprise. Put your hand firmly in His. Be open to advice from others. Seek out helpful resources such as this, and soon the fog will dissipate to reveal the path ahead. You'll begin to know what to do and how to help, and you'll reach out for your parent's hand with love and confidence. You can do this.

Chapter 1

૭૨૦

CHANGING ROLES

*Honor your father and your mother, so that you may live long
in the land the LORD your God is giving you.*

—Exodus 20:12

On one of my visits to Tennessee from Colorado to visit my mother at her assisted living community the two of us started down the hall toward the dining room for dinner. Holding on to the railing that ran along one side of the wall with her right hand, my little five-foot mom reached her left hand out to grab hold of mine. "Somehow I always feel better when you're here to hold my hand," she said, as down the hall we went.

I knew that feeling well. When I was a little girl and Mom took me downtown to shop for a new Easter dress or back-to-school shoes, I felt better when she held my hand as we crossed the busy street. Going up those big, tall steps into the school where I would start kindergarten, I couldn't have made it without her hand to steady me. All my life

I'd found security in reaching out for her and knowing she was there for me. Now she was saying, "Take my hand again," only it was my mom needing the reassurance, and I was the one being asked to find the courage and strength to provide it.

It's not like she was alone during the months between my visits. My two sisters were local and visited her frequently, and she was surrounded by other caregivers and friends in her assisted living community. But Mom liked knowing all three of her "chicks" were home to roost, and so holding my hand gave her a special sense of security.

To say I was pleased to take her hand is an understatement. But most of us, if we are honest with ourselves, are reluctant to accept the role transition such a simple gesture represents. We see signs of aging in our parents that startle or alarm us, but we dismiss them as momentary lapses or anomalies. After all, if we accept that we now must be the one to make the decisions and carry the load, then we are relinquishing the security we've always found in relying on our parents to do that.

Furthermore, how *do* we honor our fathers and mothers in this season of their lives? Do we support their wishes and desire for independence, or do we express our heartfelt concerns and insist on changes to protect their welfare? If we choose the latter, how strange that the role of caregiver and protector now becomes ours to play.

In her book *Caring for Yourself While Caring for Your Aging Parents*, Claire Berman writes about an encounter she had with a young man, an international lawyer, at a dinner party. It clearly illustrates how difficult and confusing such a change in roles can be. "The change in my mother has been very much on my mind of late," the young man said, "because the situation at my firm is no longer as stable as I'd like it to be, and I've been wondering whether to make a move. Many's the time I find myself instinctively reaching for the phone, wanting to talk to my mother about this, but then I stop myself because I realize that Mother's no longer able to support me in this way. I have found myself of late feeling a mixture of love and irritation toward my mother. She's eighty-four now, losing her grip on reality, and I have to be there for her instead of the other way around. The fact is, I want the mother I always had."[1]

This loss of the parent we always had is a long process of grief and acceptance. Where's the mom with the insightful relationship advice? Who's going to fix the leak under the sink when Dad can't? We all tend to long for the parent we are already losing, and our reluctance to accept the role transition has nothing to do with our chronological age. Some of my friends lost their mothers at a young age and were involved in their care when they were only in their twenties or thirties. A special friend of my mom's was in his eighties when his mother passed away in a nursing home, but I don't think he found it any easier to say good-bye when the time came. None of them took the caregiving role lightly nor assumed it without some denial.

Regardless of how old we are when the roles change, we just wish things could stay the way they were a bit longer. We're scared. Our aging parent is scared. We don't know if we are up to the challenge. But we're sure of one thing: in the midst of so much uncertainty, holding hands is a good idea.

Generations Together

Not so long ago in America, and in some rural areas yet today, the question of who would care for Grandma or Grandpa as they aged was predetermined. The generations shared one home, and so naturally the elder person would age in place with a loving family to care for him or her.

Until she passed away when I was sixteen, my Granny Parker lived with us. Actually, my mother and father moved into her big farmhouse in Tennessee to help her take care of the place after my grandfather passed away at a young age, so it's more accurate to say we lived with her.

I don't think my parents intended to stay for long, but they did, and as our family began to grow, we gradually took over more and more of the house. It was Granny's choice to turn most of the house over to us, but she still lived with us. Of course, the benefit of this arrangement for my sisters and me was that she was always present in our lives.

My sisters and I were never uncomfortable in the company of older people because we lived with Granny. We never had a babysitter. If my parents went out, we just stayed home with Granny. On one of those evenings, Granny played the piano and coached me through the singing of two hymns so I could try out for the school chorus. Then she made me promise not to tell anyone she could still play the piano, because she didn't want to be drafted to play for church or family events! I'm in my midsixties now, and I still think of her whenever I sing "Fairest Lord Jesus" or "This Is My Father's World."

I learned a lot about aging just hanging out with Granny playing games, reading stories, or even plucking the hair that grew out of her chin for her. Daily I observed the way my mom stepped in to drive Granny to see her friends or to the doctor. I never knew that taking care of her mother-in-law was such a sacrifice on my mom's part—because she never made it seem like one. It was simply her role to fulfill.

My times alone with Granny were intimate and authentic, and many are forever etched in my memory. A special one comes to mind as if it were yesterday. My grandmother is sitting on our screened-in back porch with a big silver bowl in her lap and a big brown bag of what we call "string beans" in Tennessee on the picnic table beside her. As I watch her snap, snap, snap, I'm lulled by the rhythm of her pace and mesmerized by the sight of her gnarled old fingers as she works.

The method Granny used was second nature to her and is now second nature to me. She snapped off each end of the bean, peeled down the string, and then gave the bean two more quick snaps in rapid succession. Snap . . . snap, zip . . . snap, snap. That's the string bean symphony.

I wondered if the bowl fit perfectly in her lap because it was made to do so, or if her lap had just molded to the shape of the bowl over the years. Always the same bowl. Always the same kind of beans.

It was on these hot summer afternoons, helping Granny snap, that I had my best talks with her. I would occasionally ask a question, knowing it could be quite a few more snaps before I got an answer. The questions were both trivial and monumental, but the answers always seemed profound.

My grandmother died two days after suffering a stroke on her ninetieth birthday. Through the years, each time I sit down with a bag of beans to snap, I feel tremendously comforted and reassured. Snapping beans gives me a feeling of connectedness that transcends time and location. My grandmother snapped beans. My mother snapped beans and threw just enough pork salt into the water when she cooked them to give them a wonderful flavor. I snap beans, too, and try to add enough spice to add the flavor without the fat—an impossible goal.

Years ago when my then two-year-old granddaughter was visiting, I encouraged her to snap string beans with me. After snapping off each end, I handed the bean to her and asked her to break it into little pieces, never dreaming she'd be able to do so without help. Her chubby little hands tightened down on the bean and she twisted it until it snapped. "Ouch!" she said, as if the snapping noise indicated the bean had been hurt. I handed her another bean. "Ouch . . . ouch!" she exclaimed as she gave it two perfect snaps.

The tears in my eyes as I watched her caught me by surprise. Now a new generation was snapping beans. Ninety-year-old, gnarled fingers . . . two-year-old pink, chubby ones . . . everything was connected. The strings that hold us together can be as simple and strong and purposeful as those on the beans. With a lot of "ouch" when they break.

The connections in family circles can still be this strong, but living together certainly makes the bonding occur more naturally. What happened to this comfortable blend of generations? When did it become the norm for grandparents to live alone or in a care center, often miles and miles away from their closest relatives? A look back may help us understand.

Looking Back

Although we tend to think that individuals are able to live longer now than ever before, that's not necessarily true. The average lifespan was indeed much shorter hundreds of years ago, but that is because many diseases back then had no immunizations or cures. Those in the eighteenth and nineteenth centuries who managed to avoid disease were as likely to live to a ripe old age as someone alive today. Now, however, so many more people are surviving that the cultural impacts are huge as we determine how to care for a much larger aging population.

The statistics are daunting. There are approximately 79 million Baby Boomers (born between 1946 and 1964) in the United States, if you include legal immigrants.[2] The first of the boomers turned sixty-five in 2011. By 2030 there will be about 72.1 million persons age sixty-five and older in the United States, more than twice the number in 2000. This means that for the first time in history, seniors will out-number children and youth.[3]

Obviously, these statistics and others are sounding an alarm to all the providers and caregivers whom seniors will look to for help to live out their days in relatively good health and comfort. They also forewarn how our elderly parents, and we, may live out the last years of life. Many in the field say we are far from ready to meet the needs of the approaching "senior tsunami." In Colorado Springs, a nonprofit collaborative titled Innovations in Aging is working to address what are seen as key factors in getting ready for the aging wave: public transportation, isolation, health care, and low-income housing.

"We believe that creating neighborhood-based resources called iHubs (intergenerational hubs) to localize information and services to support seniors in their community will reduce transportation barriers and will increase health and safety for residents," said Beth Roalstad, executive director.[4] Beth believes that communities "stepping up" are going to be crucial in the years to come—especially to fill in the gap for elders without family caregivers. Unfortunately, most communities have yet to address this growing need.

Historically, populations have approached aging with a combination of preparation and denial, much as we do today. During the Puritan era, roughly 1620–1700, there seemed to be a reverence for the elder saints of the church. Because only 2 percent of the Puritan society lived to the age of seventy, those who did were thought of as God's special people.

Throughout the early history of our country, the primary care for aging citizens remained with the family. Although we have many more institutions to assist us in this generation, those of you reading this book would no doubt agree that the primary responsibility still resides with the family, even if that looks different than it did years ago.

The first institutional homes for older people followed our nation's wars and were primarily established to care for veterans. After the Revolutionary War, Dr. Benjamin Rush, a personal friend of John and Abigail Adams, took up the cause. He also was the first to identify the onslaught of dementia in older adults.

After the Civil War, the industrial era in the United States developed so quickly that older people began to be left behind. Job seekers moved to industrial centers in hordes, and by 1920, more people lived in the city than in the country. In the 1920s and 1930s, social activism for the aging began in force, especially since older citizens suffered most from the Great Depression. It was into this social milieu that Frances Perkins, the first woman to be appointed to the US cabinet and serve as secretary of labor under Franklin D. Roosevelt, introduced the legislation that became the Social Security Act of 1935. A portion of that legislation was Old-Age, Survivors, and Disability Insurance. At the time of the act's adoption, the average life expectancy for men in the United States was fifty-eight to sixty years, and for women, sixty-two to sixty-four years. Benefits began at age sixty-five.

The ramifications of Social Security and the benefits established over the years since its inception are subjects for other discussions. Suffice it to say that you will learn more than you ever wanted to know about this program as you care for your aging family members. In addition, you will by necessity become educated about Medicare, created under Title XVIII of the Social Security Act and signed into law in 1965 by President Lyndon B. Johnson. Medicare was created to provide health insurance to people age sixty-five and older, regardless of income or medical history. Medicaid, added the same year under Title XIX of the Social Security Act, is the program that provides health insurance for individuals and families with low income and insufficient resources, including the elderly

All these programs deserve further study, and if you are in the midst of sorting out options and benefits for your aging parent, it's best to locate a professional to help you with the ins and outs. (See the recommended resources at the end of this book.) During the years my husband and I cared for my mom and his, I frequently thought of the elderly woman who I was sure existed in this country—the one without younger family members to make the phone calls, fill out the required forms, and navigate the choices these well-intentioned government programs provide. Such tasks can be beyond overwhelming for the average adult. They are nearly impossible for anyone with any level of dementia or confusion.

We've come a long way in terms of what we provide for our aging citizens in this country, and yet so much remains unchanged. The very old still need help getting to the bathroom. They still need help dressing for the day, and many need protection from a tendency to wander away unsupervised. Most need help making sound financial decisions or even balancing a checkbook. As much as some things change, so much doesn't. How we respond is the question. And the answers can vary from person to person, family to family. The answers you are looking for are the ones you hope and pray will be the right answers for your loved one, but it's so hard to be sure.

Moving Forward

While it's good to have the historical perspective, you are more concerned with how to get through this week without making the wrong decisions or frustrating the elderly person you love. Hopefully it's comforting to remember you aren't the first adult child to experience the angst that the change in roles creates. Regardless of how independently you have chosen to operate in your life and career till now, this is the time for collaboration, support, and the sharing of experiences and wisdom.

It's also a time for empathy, because just as you've never been in this position before, neither has your elder parent. Here's what author Jane Gross said about this difficult transition in her poignant, insightful book, *A Bittersweet Season: Caring for Our Aging Parents—and Ourselves*: "While it may be impossible to escape the complicated feelings engendered by being thrust into a quasi-parental role toward one's parent, you can try to leaven those thoughts by considering how *they* feel about the same role reversal. The work, and ultimately the grief, is ours, but the accretion of losses is theirs. They are giving up their independence, their physical or mental capacities, their pride, their role as head of the family, their spouses and their friends."[5]

How helpful it is for us to think of the weight of those losses on days when we yearn for a schedule of our own again, time to think, or simply time to be. Gross goes on to say, "On the days when I wished I could run away from my responsibilities, I'd practice this mind game: *If I can't bear one more day as my mother's mother, imagine how she feels.*"[6]

The losses elders suffer easily make themselves known. I was finishing up a devotional hour at an assisted living community where I volunteer when I noticed that one of the residents who had been in the class seemed a bit disoriented.

"May I help you, Sara?" I asked, to which she replied, "Well, I have a problem. I want to go home but I don't have a car. I need to call my daughter and tell her to come get me, but I don't have her number." I should have known better, having been the daughter and daughter-in-law of assisted living residents myself, but instead I suggested that she go to the office to get the number.

Very shortly she was back in the activities room with the number in hand. I offered to dial for her, handed her the phone, and heard her say, "You need to come take me home right now!" I couldn't help but overhear her daughter saying, "Mom, you are home. You live there now, remember?"

"Oh, yeah," Sara responded dejectedly. I asked her if I could speak to her daughter and she handed me the phone. I introduced myself, reassured her as best I could, and said I would see Sara safely to her room. The two of us, Sara with her cane, started the long, slow walk down one hall, then another. As we neared the room I knew was hers, I asked, "Does this look familiar, Sara?" She stopped, turned to look at me with tears in her eyes, and said, "Yes. But I don't like it."

Always my favorite resident to visit until she passed away, and the subject of many more joyful stories, Sara gradually adjusted to her losses and the transition that gave her daughter the role of decision-maker regarding her welfare. But it was an agonizing period of adjustment for both of them.

Accepting the change in roles must always precede the ability to move forward in a way that is both caring and productive for all involved. Otherwise, we are simply stuck with our roles frozen in time. The signs that we have to step in, that the roles must indeed shift, are as individual as the older adults for whom we collectively care.

Pam's mother lived in Canada while Pam was miles away in the United States. She first began to suspect a change was necessary when a visit revealed that her mom, then in her nineties, was having difficulty remembering appointments and assimilating important information. "Mom was always a voracious and informed reader," Pam said, "so I was taken aback when on one visit books and other items were in the same place that I had left them two months before. She always made detailed notes of everything, but now the notes were so touchingly sad and repetitive, and showed such an internal struggle as she tried unsuccessfully to make everything seem stable."

Gail was thrust into a caregiving role with both her mom and her dad in a neighboring state, but the beginnings of the transition in roles looked different with each parent. "My mother's dementia became obvious when I couldn't get a clear answer regarding the results of her doctor appointments or information about her prescriptions," Gail said. "Also, my normally chatty mother was keeping our phone conversations very short, asking only general questions about the kids, work, and the weather. She was afraid that if she talked more her dementia would be obvious to me—and to her, so she stayed away from specifics."

While Gail's mom tried to cover up her dementia, her dad was open about his encroaching Alzheimer's. "When my father turned eighty, he honestly told me that he thought he had the beginnings of Alzheimer's. He said he would forget why he was in a room, what he was going to do next, or where he placed something," Gail remembered. "While it was a surprise to me that Dad was admitting it, he wasn't overly concerned; he reminded me that after all, he was eighty!"

Two very different ways of getting the news. But they were equally concerning to an out-of-state, married daughter with three children and a high-powered job. No matter how you come to realize that your life is about to change dramatically, it can be an adjustment at first. So we remember that it's even harder for our elder parent, and we move forward one day at a time.

A poignant essay by Virginia Wells appeared in an issue of *Ladies' Home Journal* and speaks volumes about the role transition with her mom. She begins with a memory of herself as a little girl watching her mother get ready to go out for the evening: "My mother stands at the bathroom mirror putting on makeup. She has delicate hands with slim fingers and nails painted Revlon Fire & Ice red. She smoothes on foundation, then rouge and a little eye color. Finally, she takes lipstick, Fire & Ice too, carefully outlines her lips, then presses them together. She pulls me close and kisses me hard on the mouth. She's a sweet mixture of soap and cologne. Together, we look at our reflection. Now I am wearing lipstick too."

Many years later the reflection is quite different. "My mother has a fractured ankle and she has stayed with me for several weeks," she writes. "She can barely use a walker, but she tries, her shoulders stooped over as she inches her way across the room. She's quiet; she has nothing to say. . . . One night I sit her in front of the mirror and find my own Fire & Ice polish. I hold her thin fingers in mine and spread the color evenly over her nails. My mother watches as her pale hands come alive. For a moment I realize that she is still in there somewhere, and I know I will stay close by, waiting till she reappears."[7]

Maybe this story touches my heart so deeply because I can still see my own mother's gorgeous nails adorned with Revlon's Windsor Rose (since discontinued). I wore a similar shade before she died but haven't been able to use it since. It's enough that my hands look just like hers even without the polish. One of many ways I am so much like my mother, and so, never truly without her.

Accepting the Call

In the well-loved Bible study *Experiencing God*, authors Henry T. Blackaby and Claude V. King remind readers that answering God's call on their lives will always require making major adjustments. "Every time God spoke to people in the Scripture about something He wanted to do through them, major adjustments were necessary," they write. "They had to adjust their lives to God. Once the adjustments were made, God accomplished His purposes through those He called."[8] Once you sense the call to help your aging parent, those words will be true of you as well. This may be one of the most significant calls you will ever receive. And the sacrifices you and your family have to make in order for you to answer the call will soon be evident.

The call might not come as clearly as the one you get in the middle of the night alerting you to a crisis in an elderly person's life. It may be a gentle nudging of the Holy Spirit that the responsibility for a loved one's care is being placed on your shoulders. Part of accepting the call is recognizing its uniqueness. Your siblings may be hearing that they are to serve their parents in a much different way than you are, or it may seem as if they are escaping responsibility altogether. This doesn't change your call, and the fact that you're reading this book is one indication that the call may be yours.

Celebrity Robin Roberts was diagnosed with a rare blood disorder following breast cancer treatment that required her to go into the hospital for a bone marrow transplant. She assumed that her closest sibling, Dorothy, would be the match, but it turned out to be her sister Sally-Ann. As Robin and Sally-Ann began the process of preparing for the transplant, their mother, Lucimarian, was close to death in her home in Pass Christian, Mississippi. It was Dorothy who was able to be with their mother. She was the one who received the call at that time.

Yet certainly celebrities are often called into duty as caregivers. Singer Amy Grant, interviewed on the talk show hosted by Katie Couric, shared tips she learned from taking care of her parents. She recommends starting the conversation about care early, saying, "Let us know what you want. You trained us for this; you did your job well." Other tips included taking healthy meals by to combat poor nutrition as well as playing games requiring physical movement. "There's a lot of joy in it," she says of caring for elders. "You are gonna cry, but you're gonna laugh."[9]

Likewise, former *Good Morning America* anchor Joan Lunden became actively involved with caring for her mom. Deciding where her mother should live was "one of the more emotionally trying experiences I have faced," Lunden said. She is now a spokesperson for a service that helps families make these decisions, A Place for Mom (www.aplaceformom.com).

When I asked my friend Gail, who cared for both her aging parents from a distance, if she had any advice to give others embarking on a similar journey, she said, "It gets easier once you tell yourself 'this is hard, but I'm going to have to settle in and go through it.' It's only for a season. If you embrace it, with all the ups and downs, you will feel a richness and deeper sense of purpose. You will know that in your own way you are completing the circle of life." My friend Kathy put the same advice a slightly different way: "Love much. Die to your personal comfort for a season—it's worth it. Honor your father and mother."

There are few times in life when we can be absolutely sure our heavenly Father is looking down on us with delight and approval. All of them seem to involve self-sacrifice and reaching out to others. If you are hearing the call to care for an aging loved one, embrace it and adjust your life accordingly. And by the way, you don't have to be a blood relative to hear the call. My friend Shar did everything a loving daughter would have done for her older friend Jeanne, right up to holding Jeanne's hand when she died. She heard the call to meet the needs of a dear woman who had no one else to turn to, and she responded.

It won't be easy to respond to the call, and you may not always feel appreciated, but the rewards for you and your loved one will be rich indeed. In fact, they will be eternal.

Chapter 2

❧

KNOWING WHAT TO DO

We do not know what to do, but our eyes are upon you.
—2 Chronicles 20:12

My mother-in-law slides her still statuesque frame across the seat of the booth at Red Lobster, excited to indulge in the once-a-week repast she enjoys when she goes there with us: clam chowder and a glass of Chardonnay. My husband reaches around her to help her take off her coat, and as her arm emerges from the sleeve, we both gasp.

"Mom, what are those bruises?" Jim asks.

"Oh, that. It's probably just where I fell into the wall," she replies offhandedly. "What are you going to order?"

These are massive bruises running from her elbow down to her wrist. We can't leave the subject unexplored, but it soon becomes obvious that Mary Frances has no interest in discussing what happened to her arm. People fall; they get bruises. Next topic, please.

Signs that it may be time for a change in an older person's living situation may be even more obvious than our experience. Of the stories I've heard, let me share a few.

Every evening, Carol Ann pours herself a cool beverage, puts her purse on her arm, and goes from door to door in her neighborhood ringing doorbells and asking if anyone there is watching *Antiques Roadshow*. If so, she'd like to come in! The neighbors have been very kind to her so far, but this can't go on.

Richard, who knew his landlady was sending the carpet cleaners to his apartment to deal with the consequences of his bathroom accidents, opened the door to the carpet man stark naked.

And then there's Margot, now ninety-five, a woman with an amazing history. As a young German in her midtwenties, she spent two and a half years sampling Hitler's food to make sure it wasn't poisoned. Her survival inspires everyone who hears her story. But now, due to her age and the absence of an elevator, Margot has not left her Berlin apartment building in eight years.[1] Can this be right? Who deserves to feel the sun on her face and hear the birds singing more than Margot?

Sometimes the indications that a change is needed are more subtle. The signs that let my sisters know my mom was in trouble were more emotional than physical. Usually when one of them called my mom to say, "I'll swing by and get you and we'll go get a burger," she'd respond with, "Great, what time?" But when months went by and she always had an excuse for not accepting any of their invitations, they knew something was seriously wrong. The times they dropped by the house, she was likely curled up on her couch with the TV on, books and magazines left untouched on the coffee table. Even the daily papers seemed to pile up without her usual careful perusal.

From over a thousand miles away, I heard the concern in my sisters' voices when I asked them, "How's Mom?" And when I talked to my mother, it always seemed like she was in a hurry to get off the phone. For decades, her approach had been not to worry me with anything that was wrong with her, since I "lived so far away and couldn't do anything about it anyway." She would implore my sisters not to tell me when she needed minor surgery or tests, saying, "Now, don't worry Nancy with this. We'll call her when it's all over." This well-intended attitude protected me from worry but ultimately left me feeling painfully out of touch. Yet even from my distant, protected perspective, I began to sense, if not see, the cracks in her façade when she began slipping into depression. When I learned she wasn't even going to church anymore, I knew she was in trouble.

Obviously there's no pat checklist of signs that will let an adult child know beyond a shadow of a doubt that an elderly parent needs intervention and help. As with most of life, our instincts tell us the most. Combining instincts with tears and prayers for guidance, eventually the situation comes into clear focus, and in time the solutions present themselves.

Sometimes the signs are progressive. Are the falls more frequent or more injurious? Are you no longer able to connect with your parent by phone on a regular basis? Does your parent appear to be losing both appetite and weight, and show little interest in cooking? If he or she does cook, do you worry about kitchen fires—or have there been some? If your parent is still driving, are there signs you should be concerned for his or her safety or the safety of others? Are you afraid your parent isn't taking his or her medications? Have you noticed that the house isn't as clean as it used to be—or does it have an odor? Is your parent making questionable financial decisions? These are just some of the more obvious signs that it's time to at least ask your elder if it's time for a change.

The Talk

In the best of situations, Baby Boomer adults will have "the talk" with their parents about a change in their living situation long before a decision has to be made. Many of us haven't had a conversation with our parents so packed with tension since they sat us down to tell us where babies come from.

There are many reasons why this conversation gets postponed. For one, it is difficult and feels somewhat disrespectful. After all, our parents are and always will be our parents; no role reversal takes place in that regard. Also, old parent-child dynamics, including unresolved issues in the relationship, may raise their ugly heads. And siblings may disagree on what needs to be said and when, and it therefore isn't possible for the adult children to present a unified position. Add distance, fear of rejection, and lack of preparation to the mix and you can readily understand why "the talk" may not go well the first time it occurs—or even the second time.

As I write, my husband and I are in our midsixties. We would like to think that we are eons away from having a difficult conversation with one or all of our four children about our ability to live on our own, but one guideline for when the talk needs to take place is that the grown children are forty or more and the seniors are seventy or more.

Oh, really? I would love to assume, especially given my study of gerontology, that we will be gracious and amenable when our children broach the subject of our ability to continue on as we are, but somehow I doubt we will. Wasn't it just yesterday that we were waiting up for these same kids to get home with the car? Who are these upstarts to question whether we should be driving or living on our own?

Once you put yourself in your elder parent's place, the conversation may not be any easier, but you'll certainly go into it with a more empathetic heart.

In truth, it's not just one talk you need to have but several. Even before the question of moving to a safer environment comes up, it's wise to discuss the topics that *RealSimple* magazine outlined in an article titled "5 Tough Parental Talks."[2] They suggest using questions as a way to broach these sensitive topics. I would add that holding hands and praying together before beginning would help to unify your hearts and minds, and asking God for His insight into the situation is never fruitless.

First, *do you have a will?* Without one, assets can be tied up in probate court, and there's no guarantee that belongings will be distributed the way the deceased person would wish. To bring this up, consider saying something like, "I don't want to upset you, but if something happened to you, I would want to know that your wishes were being honored. Do you have a will?"

Second, *do you have a power of attorney?* This designation gives another party the ability to make legal and financial decisions in the event that a person is unable to do so. The approach might sound something like this: "Mom, I want someone designated to make my decisions for me in an emergency, so I'm getting my paperwork together. I would feel so much better if you did the same."

Third, *do you have advance health care directives?* These usually include a living will detailing instructions on life-sustaining measures, a health proxy giving someone else the right to make medical decisions on the person's behalf, and a HIPPA release, a document allowing access to medical records. Having these in place protects families from arguments or lawsuits. You might say, "If you were ever on life support, I would be really torn up and not in the best frame of mind to make a decision. I know we talked about how you feel, but I think it would give both of us some relief if you put it into writing."

Fourth, and perhaps the most testy, *do you have an authorized user on your bank and investment accounts?* This is necessary in order to access your parent's funds to cover such expenses as medical care, a care center, or funeral arrangements. Try saying, "Dad, I'm not trying to take over your money, but there are a few documents that would let me handle your finances just in case I ever needed to. Can we talk about them?"

Fifth, *have you thought about long-term care insurance?* While not the right choice for everyone, it can help defray the cost of in-home or nursing home care. To bring this up, consider saying, "I read about how much assisted living can cost, and I was stunned. I would want you to have the best care if it came to that. Have you looked into insurance?"[3]

These aren't all the topics you want to discuss with your aging parents, but certainly they provide guidelines we would all be wise to follow. And once these steps have been taken, the move into a care center, with the increased level of involvement from adult children such a move dictates, will go much more smoothly.

The Generation Gap

One barrier that is hard to overcome when communicating with our aging parents is that we come from different generations—generations that were molded by vastly different world experiences, technology, and yes, sometimes even by different values. Those who were born and grew up in the early part of the twentieth century experienced two World Wars and a Great Depression. They learned to make the best of whatever situation they found themselves in. They appreciated everything they had and, for the most part, were taught not to complain or whine.

Our parents' generation, often called the Greatest Generation, saw incredible changes in their lifetime, and they rolled with those changes. They worked hard to make sure their children (us) would have a higher standard of living than they had. Who among us didn't hear admonishments from our parents such as, "Rise above it." "Pull yourself up by your bootstraps and get on with it." Or, "If at first you don't succeed, try, try again." We may get frustrated with our parents' lack of flexibility, but their stubbornness and determination may be the very things that made it possible for them to live so long in the first place. Not ones to overanalyze things or go in for a lot of psychobabble, the Greatest Generation survived by their own wits and efforts, and any other approach was seen as less than admirable.

Sitting across the kitchen table from them are we, the Baby Boomers. We don't have the same sense of entitlement as the generations that follow us, but we do feel entitled to direct our future. We've been trained to be proactive: to have a vision and a strategic plan not only for our businesses but also for our churches and our private lives.

We like to anticipate what's coming and get ready for it. We're comfortable with outsourcing when necessary and with calling in experts to gather information on every aspect of life. And maybe, just maybe, we tend to "worry a thing to death," as our parents may be quick to point out. No wonder there's a gap that must be bridged before real conversation about such a difficult subject as our parents' giving up their independence can occur.

Experts say the best approach for talking about this sensitive subject may be to simply take advantage of the natural opportunities that occur to broach the subject over a period of years, using non-threatening questions rather than statements or directives. For instance, if you are taking your mom to the funeral of one of her friends, the third friend to die in a year, ask her if she is lonely and ever wonders what it would be like to live with your family or in a community of others her age. When someone she knows moves into assisted living, ask her if she'd like to go visit and then make the arrangements. If she decides to tour the facility while she's there, so much the better. If you get the call that she has fallen and you come to take her to the doctor, ask if she worries about being alone or not being able to reach someone after a fall. This could also be the perfect time to suggest that she subscribe to a medical alert system that provides immediate help when the button in a pendant worn around the neck is pushed. So often this is the first step elderly parents agree to—mostly for their children's peace of mind if not their own.

Of course we learned the hard way that this system isn't foolproof. The time my mother-in-law fell in the bathroom in the middle of the night, her pendant was on her bedside table. She had rolled over on it once and made it go off accidentally, so she decided she'd just take it off when she went to bed so that wouldn't happen again.

My mother had the opposite problem. Her button once went off, and when no one could reach her by phone, the service sent the police and an ambulance to her house. My sisters both got emergency calls too, so they rushed to the house, sure that my mother had fallen victim to the rash of carjackings occurring in the area. Imagine my mother's surprise when she drove up the driveway to see all those people! She had simply gone to Shoney's for all-you-can-eat fish night, but because she was only five feet tall and had the car seat moved as far forward as it would go, the steering wheel had pressed against her pendant and sent out the alarm. No wonder some elders declare such services a prime example of "much ado about nothing," more of a bother than a help.

Lack of control of our own lives is scary for us at any age, so the best approach to having the talk about future care may be to boldly bring up the subject but leave the next steps up to your elder. Consider asking your dad, "How will you know when it's time to change your living situation? What factors will you consider when you make the decision? Is there any information you still need that I could gather for you?" Such questions open the conversation while leaving the elder person in charge of his or her own future, as it should be.

Our aging parents may have some of the same concerns we have even though they haven't verbalized them. For every fall we know about, they may know about ten. For every sign of confusion we see, they may have experienced a hundred. They know, even if they can't seem to broach the conversation themselves.

You'll know when it's time to talk. And if you find the generation gap too wide, consider asking a trusted doctor or pastor—or an adored adult grandchild—to be the bridge. Of the three, don't dismiss the grandchild too quickly. Often a bond develops between grandparents and grandkids that is based on more than love: both groups have to deal with whom they perceive to be the controlling generation in between (that would be us). An elder may find it easier to accept the truth from the lips of a precious grandchild whose only motivation is love than from an adult child who seems to be acting way too bossy lately. If grandchildren are willing and comfortable with the assignment, let them have a go at it.

Deciding with Siblings

The experience of caring for an aging parent is replete with circle-of-life experiences. Many are obvious: we who were the children become the adults; those we looked up to now have to be cared for by us as we take their hands again.

Yet in some ways, the circle-of-life experience is more subtle. So it is with coming to agreement with siblings about what needs to be done for a parent. Due to circumstances beyond our control, we are forced to progress around the circle to a position where we can respond to the situation as adults, not as children, and this isn't always easy.

Just as good parents discuss their disagreements about child rearing and discipline out of their children's hearing, so adult siblings need to work through any disagreements about the care of their mom or dad out of earshot of the elders they love. More than anything, parents want their children to get along, and if they think they are the source of conflict for any reason, that can be the cruelest blow of all. Disagree elsewhere, come to a consensus, and present a unified front—just as you would when rearing children.

Disagreements arise for many reasons. Personality types come into play. So do factors like risk aversion. And of course there's geography. Adult children who live close to a parent may resent a distant sibling's expressing the opinion that more care is needed when the lion's share of that extra care will fall on the nearby family members. Conversely, distant siblings may believe the closer siblings are exaggerating the situation. They may believe it's not necessary to rock the boat because, as far as they can tell, things are going quite smoothly according to what dad says on the phone each Sunday. Clearly, communication between siblings is the key to arriving at an approach to which all can agree.

My husband and I were both blessed to have siblings who were good partners in making decisions and caring for our aging moms. We also had a chance to see the challenges from two different perspectives: up close and personal through our hands-on involvement with Jim's mom, and trying to help from a distance with my mom. Each situation presented its own difficulties, its own rewards, and its own way of partnering with siblings.

Yet others don't find sibling relationships helpful for a variety of reasons. Initially, discord may come from an eruption of feelings such as, "Mom always liked you best" or "Dad never would listen to me." Many families are able to move past that point quickly when the welfare of a beloved parent is in the balance. Others need help coming to a consensus.

At the Aging Center at the University of Colorado in Colorado Springs, Dr. Sara Qualls and her colleagues counsel entire families as part of the process of deciding next steps for an aging loved one. "We need to understand the entire family as a context for helping the caregiver," Dr. Qualls told me in a personal interview.[4] "We need to understand the family structure so we can help the caregiver structure care appropriately. We also want to make sure that as many family members as possible understand the needs and the goals and are okay with the change, so there is less backlash against decisions the caregiver must make."

Making unilateral decisions when siblings disagree complicates things and will delay the care of the person you desperately want to help. It's important to delay any major decision until all siblings are on board—or agree to pretend to be for the sake of their parent. Do whatever it takes to mutually determine a course of action.

When There's No Choice

Having a choice about the direction an elderly person's life will take is a privilege not all are given. Often a crisis precipitates the discussion about a change in care, and many decisions have to be made quickly, without the luxury of research or adjustment on anyone's part. Dad's Alzheimer's sends him wandering the neighborhood, utterly disoriented. Or Mom falls and breaks a hip (or breaks a hip and then falls, as is often the case). In such instances, decisions have to be made quickly, at least in terms of meeting the loved one's immediate needs.

This was the case with Naomi, a lovely, elegant octogenarian whom I met in the assisted living community where I volunteer. "I was at home living my life, and the next thing I knew, I was living here. It was a lot to get used to," she told me. She had been hospitalized, and her only child, a daughter who had flown in from California, felt it necessary to arrange a safe place for her mother to live. Things progressed ahead of Naomi's comfort level, and it took her months to adjust to her new surroundings.

The decision-making process is a balancing act between concerns about the elderly person's health and safety on one hand and freedom of choice and independence on the other. Ultimately the decision belongs to the elder we are trying to help. We can't force our parents to do the responsible thing in their old age any more than they could force us not to drink and drive in college or use birth control when we had sex. We knew what was right, but we made our own choices.

My husband and I knew that my mother-in-law's choice to stay in her own home was fraught with harmful possibilities, but the trade-off was her happiness and independence—and it was difficult to convince her to do anything she didn't want to do. Her strongest argument, often delivered, was that because of her macular degeneration, she was safer in a familiar environment. In her own home of fifty years, she knew where every light switch was and knew every piece of furniture to avoid. Although she had fallen and broken both wrists, gone to a rehab hospital, and then returned home, her argument was a reasonable one, so we acquiesced to her desire to stay in her home with care, knowing full well she could fall down the stairs someday. She did. But the quality of her life those two years she was able to return to her home was much better than the quality of life she had later. To her, it was worth both the risk of the fall and the fall. And wasn't that her choice to make?

My own mother's path to a decision was less clear-cut. Once she became almost incapacitated by her depression, and her psychiatrist insisted she shouldn't be left alone but needed more socialization, she went to live with my sister Patty. Patty, who had mobility and health issues of her own, waited on my mom hand and foot. Mom meanwhile kept insisting that she wasn't ready for assisted living. But as the days turned into weeks, we finally had to tell her, "You are in assisted living now, only it's Patty providing the care, and she can't go on doing all she is doing for you without risking her own health."

Mom would never have wanted to make life harder for any of her three daughters, so she agreed to move into assisted living, taking just the clothes she had with her. As Patty said, "It's as if she went there on vacation and never came home."

Both of our moms "backed into" their decisions to move out of their longtime homes, and I want to honor their memories by granting them a lot of grace for the routes they took. Both lost their husbands at an early age and then lived another lifetime as widows. The homes they had loved in, entertained in, reared children in, and made a million meals in, continued to fill up with an accumulation of lives well-lived. It was overwhelming for them to do the sorting necessary to make a move, and they wouldn't accept help cleaning out either. Each of them said, "You can just deal with it when I'm gone." Yet stories also abound of folks who systematically downsize their belongings and square footage decade by decade, and then rationally announce to their adult children when they are ready to move into a care facility.

What makes some elders able to embrace change while others fight it or deny the need for it for all they're worth? It's impossible to know. The experiences elders had caring for their own parents may shape their thinking. Those who move on more easily may have a strong sense of pragmatism and, just maybe, the desire to maintain control, or what's known as "the pride of self-direction," during this most difficult transition period of their lives. But while the progression from independent living to a care facility can take a practical, progressive path, it didn't in our family and may not in yours.

So how will you know it's time for a change? You just will. My

Granny Parker always wore a navy blue sweater. Unfortunately, she wore this favorite sweater long after the elbows were worn through, the buttons were missing, and the cuffs were stretched out of shape. After she passed away at age ninety, we found four brand-new navy blue sweaters in the bottom drawer of her dresser, still wrapped in their original tissue paper. We could give her new sweaters, but we couldn't make her wear them.

Trying to keep and care for elders we love in the home they love can feel as futile as patching up an old sweater. We darn one hole and another materializes. We replace one button and another falls off. Eventually it's just time to give up and go with a new sweater.

We can put up rails in the bathroom, screw in brighter lightbulbs, pick up slippery throw rugs, arrange for meal deliveries, subscribe to a medical alert service, schedule alternate transportation, commit to regular visits and phone calls, and on and on. But eventually the time comes when we and the ones we love so much must admit, "this isn't working anymore." That's when you know it's time for a change. That's when you hold hands, ask the Lord's guidance, and take the next step together.

Chapter 3

༺

DECIDING WHERE MY PARENT WILL LIVE

Jesus replied, "Foxes have holes and birds of the air have nests,
but the Son of Man has no place to lay his head."

—Matthew 8:20

Some words spoken during a crisis can engrave themselves on our hearts and reside in our memories long afterward. My mother said many sweet things to my sisters and me during her lifetime, but as we prepared to help her move into the assisted living facility that eventually became her home, she said, "I can't believe you want me to lay my head down in some strange place night after night."

I don't think I remembered to tell her that Jesus said He didn't have a place to lay his Head at all, but I'm not sure it would have mattered at that time. We all know how much we cherish crawling into our own beds at the end of a long day. And no matter how fancy the surroundings or how high the thread counts of the sheets in a hotel room, we all sleep better once we return from a trip and collapse onto our own bed. Of course, it's more than the bed. It's the whole environment we find comforting: the way the light comes in through the window in the morning and the sound of the birds in the trees outside. If we're blessed to be happily married, it's also the familiarity of the warm body next to us and the rhythmic sound of our spouse's breathing. Elders who have lost spouses may cherish the comfort of a familiar bed in a familiar setting, and the memories both evoke, more than we can imagine unless we experience such loss.

So we must begin the journey toward a new living arrangement for a beloved elder with the understanding that whatever we and our elders choose, it won't feel like home to them—at least not at first. Even moving the same bed to a different location won't take away the angst and sense of loss.

If ever there is a time in your life when you need to humble yourself, realize you don't know everything, call on the opinions of experts, and tap into the resources available, this is it. Before you know which level of care to recommend you need to know exactly where your parents stand physically and mentally and combine this information with their personal preferences. Only then will you be ready to determine how their needs can best be met.

First, the physical assessment. No one will be more valuable to you at this time than a physician who practices geriatrics or at least has a significant number of seniors in his or her practice. If you have a physician who has treated your mom or dad for a long time, and thus been a trusted advisor for years, so much the better.

Second, it's necessary to get a neurological assessment in order to uncover any element of dementia or other cognitive decline that needs to be considered. Very accurate, simple, noninvasive tests have been developed for use in this assessment. If your doctor's office or local hospital cannot recommend someone to provide this service, search for a community center on aging or other senior organization near you. Chances are, they will provide the service at little or no cost or refer you to someone who can. Relying solely on your own observations or that of siblings, and on your elder's self-evaluation of how he or she does cognitively, is simply not enough. Call in the experts and get the facts.

Once you have gathered all the data you can, you're ready to sort through the options of where your loved one should live. Remember, many middle-aged adults have traveled this road before you, so don't be too proud to ask for their opinions and referrals. Most will be more than willing to make the journey easier for you than it was for them. Services like A Place for Mom (www.aplaceformom.com) are also available to assist you in sorting through options. If your loved one is in the midst of a health crisis, you'll need to come up with a short-term solution, even if it means taking your elder home with you in order to buy time before making an informed decision about long-term care. (This can also be a long-term solution, as we will discuss later.) Remember, it's not unusual for some facilities to have waiting lists, so patience may be required.

Levels of Care: What's the Difference?

What are the options once you have determined that a change in living arrangements is necessary? The continuum ranges from "aging in place," with additional help, all the way to twenty-four-hour advanced nursing care and/or memory care. As with any journey into unknown territory, it helps to familiarize yourself with the lay of the land and the language spoken there—or in this case, the terminology used to delineate one level of care from another. It's also important to know that what's "just right" for your elder at one point in time may not be adequate later, so a regular reassessment is a must.

The levels of care are as follows.

Aging in Place: In your aging parent's heart and in yours, this is where you hope the decision-making process leads you. National franchises like Interim HealthCare, Right at Home, Visiting Angels, Home

Instead, etc., advertise their home health care services as the perfect solution for seniors who need just a little extra help with cleaning, shopping, or hygiene, or who simply want some companionship. Often this is an important interim step, as it was for my mother-in-law.

These organizations in your area are only as good as the people they hire, so if this is your choice, interview carefully and drop in often if possible to see how things are going. If your elder doesn't connect with his or her caregiver for any reason, don't hesitate to ask for a replacement; not all of these workers are like the ones on the national ads. Also, watch for any unexplained expenditures, as seniors are often victims of financial abuse.

Cost: Check with local providers. Most workers are paid an hourly rate.

Independent Communities: Often the best choice for older couples blessed to be going through their later years together is the fifty-five-plus independent senior community. Residents lease or own their own stand-alone or attached homes but can take advantage of recreation, transportation, and dining options provided by the community. Such places offer scheduled daily activities and a higher level of security, safety, and stability than the elders may have had in their previous homes, bringing peace of mind to residents and to their concerned adult children. Usually home maintenance and lawn care are also provided.

Benefits include being able to choose between cooking in or eating in the dining room and between driving or taking community transportation. Making friends with other residents may happen more easily in these communities, and residents enjoy as much privacy and independence as they want.

Cost: Varies with real estate markets. It will be higher than a similar residence in a regular neighborhood due to community amenities.

Assisted Living Communities: Once it's determined that a senior needs daily assistance with activities like bathing, dressing, eating, transferring from chair to bed, toileting, or walking, it's time to consider an assisted living facility.

These facilities are only as good as the aides who come in and out of the rooms. I began praying that if the aides helping my mother and mother-in-law weren't particularly intelligent or skilled, they would at least have a good heart. You can't buy compassion. It's there or it isn't.

If you are concerned your mom or dad may literally or figuratively get lost in one of the huge assisted living complexes, you may want to look for a resident home that provides all the services of assisted living but limits occupancy to six to twelve residents.

Cost: Monthly rates vary depending on location and level of care.

Skilled Nursing Facilities: This is the new, politically correct term for nursing homes. (Industry insiders refer to SNFs as "sniffs," and yes, I had to ask what that term meant when I heard it tossed around.) The concept is the same. Facilities must follow strict state and federal guidelines which mandate that they provide twenty-four-hour certified nursing assistance, LPNs, and RNs. Usually the accommodations are smaller than assisted living apartments, frequently with two residents to a room. When your loved one needs constant care, this is the best choice, but unfortunately some of the reports of abuse and neglect our elders remember hearing about in the old-style nursing homes still exist, so choose carefully.

Cost: Rates are per day, based on location and use of Medicare or Medicaid.

Memory Care: Elders with advanced dementia or Alzheimer's need constant care and may or may not also have physical conditions requiring attention. Memory care facilities, often just separate wings within an assisted living facility, provide a safe environment for those with advanced memory loss who exhibit difficult behaviors such as excessive wandering inside and outside of the building. It's tough to accept that your loved one is being kept behind locked doors and monitored twenty-four hours a day, but if this level of care becomes necessary, then you will also be extremely grateful for it.

Cost: Definitely in the higher range of assisted living cost due to the vigilance required by staff.

While one level of care may seem perfect at the time the initial decision is made, that can change in a heartbeat. We saw this clearly with my mother-in-law. Thank goodness for the physician who sat us down in the midst of our shock and confusion and told us, "It's common for seniors to cycle through the system from one type of care to another. After a hospital stay, they go to skilled nursing for rehabilitation, then to assisted living. They stay there until the next health crisis and then start through the cycle again."

This was our reality. After falling and breaking both wrists, my mother-in-law went from the hospital to a skilled nursing facility. Once she was well enough and had the rods in her arms removed, she want back home with home health care, where she stayed for two years until she fell down the stairs. Then she moved into assisted living, where she stayed until she broke her hip. She then went back into the hospital, cycled back into skilled nursing, and then passed away before completing the cycle back into assisted living.

Some say there's a way to make this cycling easier on everyone. One of your options, as you explore various senior communities, may be the "continuum care campus," which claims to provide a single location for every level of care. Residents can move from independent living to assisted living to skilled nursing as their needs require. Some campuses even include hospitals.

The benefit of having all levels of care offered in one place is that you and your elder don't have to go through the agony of finding a new location and moving each time a new level of care is needed. That, at least, is the theory. In reality, the move from one level of care to another may not be as seamless and easy as presented by the marketing representative who takes you on the tour. Accommodations may not be available in the next level of care when your loved one requires them, and the transition can be problematic.

Moving Mary Frances from her assisted living apartment to a skilled nursing room within the same building, not just the same campus, was like moving her from Earth to Mars. Rather than transfer all the information on file in the assisted living wing to skilled nursing, the facility required that we start from scratch filling out forms, listing medications, and so on. It was *not* a seamless transfer. And since the staff was completely different on the skilled nursing side of the building, there was no continuity of relationships.

How Will We Know Our Choice Is OK?

We've all seen the ads on TV. Well-dressed, happy seniors are shown toasting one another with glasses of wine, strolling through well-kept gardens, and reading in beautiful living rooms. Those are the same scenes you will see on the brochures of the facilities you visit. But how do you find out what it's really like to live there—before you ask someone you love as much as anyone on earth to move in?

Never mind what a facility's marketing/PR representative or executive director tells you about quality of care or activities. The programs and accreditations may sound wonderful, but what matters to your senior is the level of care and concern he or she will receive. And that is determined far more by the people who are employed there than by the national corporation touting the latest in eldercare amenities. Will the aide who comes into the room have a compassionate, patient attitude? Will information and special requests be communicated from one shift to the next?

If time permits you the luxury of making an informed decision, ask for references from families who have used the services of the facility you are considering. If possible, talk to them privately over the phone or in person. Talk to pastors and doctors who visit facilities in your community often, and ask them where they would or wouldn't take their own mothers. They often see things other people wouldn't.

It's a good idea to pay at least two visits to a facility: one that is scheduled and the other, unscheduled. Also, ask for a schedule of activities, and drop by during one of the appointed times to see if the activity is actually happening and people are participating. Eat a meal or two in the dining room—with residents, if possible. And look for opportunities to casually chat with lower-level employees. Do they seem disgruntled and unhappy? That translates into neglect and high turnover.

What do the residents say? If you have a chance, ask them what they enjoy most about where they are living and what they would change if they could. As the Caring.com article "What You Can Expect from a Great Assisted Living Community" states, "It's not the indoor heated pools or fitness rooms that make for a good assisted living community—it's when your loved one knows she belongs. It's when a staff member notices that something just isn't right and your loved one receives prompt attention. It's when other residents smile when they see her step into the dining room, or when you, the family member, know you can stop by any time."[1]

The article goes on to list five things all excellent assisted living communities have in common, and what each means to the resident: a clean, safe place where needs are addressed promptly; homey touches; a trustworthy staff; great amenities; and a family-friendly atmosphere.

Choosing a safe and caring skilled nursing facility can be even more challenging than choosing an assisted living community. And monitoring the ongoing care can be extremely difficult. In assisted living, most residents (unless they suffer from dementia) are able to let family members know if their needs are not being met or if they are being neglected or abused in any way. Skilled nursing facility residents, on the other hand, may be helplessly bedridden, and some may not be able to communicate well enough to let loved ones know what happens when they are left there alone.

Unfortunately, neglect and abuse still occur. But we are blessed to have regulations and watchdog groups for skilled nursing facilities.

Any investigation conducted will probably appear if you search the facility by name online, so take advantage of that information. Also, Medicare.gov offers an online comparison feature that shows each facility's star ratings in three categories and in overall quality, with five stars being the highest rating. You won't regret any time you spend researching before making your decision.

Regardless of how confident you are of the decision you and your elder make, there's no substitute for being an active advocate for your loved one. If you don't live close enough to drop by frequently, it's worth finding someone who will, even if you have to hire a professional advocate. Remember, this is the generation who grew up not complaining about anything and not wanting to "be a bother." So assuming that everything is going well just because you desperately want it to may not be the best approach.

Creative Housing Solutions

Necessity is indeed the mother of invention—and desperation may be the father. Elders who can't imagine being happy with any of the traditional options may encourage their sons and daughters to think outside the box. Listen carefully to their accounts of living situations they've heard about and find enticing. After all, they didn't live to their age without being resourceful.

In The New Old Age blog in the *New York Times* (an excellent resource for anyone needing to take their parents' hands again), author Paula Span writes about her father's South Jersey apartment building, which is essentially a naturally occurring retirement community (NORC).[2] Although people of all ages live in the building, a significant number of residents have grown old there together. Over the years, they've learned to rely on one another for transportation, help when they are ill, and daily companionship. Paula's dad, Murray, is the one who buys the daily newspaper and circulates it around the lobby in the afternoons. But all the elders there have a special niche to fill.

So popular are these spontaneous senior residences that twenty-five states have funded NORC-supportive service programs that provide on-site nursing and banking services. Some even provide social service workers to help with tasks like bill paying, exercise classes, book groups, and field trips—in other words, many of the same services offered in the more expensive assisted living communities.[3]

Here's another creative solution. A couple ready for a retirement home decided they could live much more comfortably and affordably in an economy motel. Getting the monthly rate, they made their comfortable room—featuring attached bath, cable TV, and free wireless—their new home. Public transportation was right out the door, and laundry service was provided daily. Breakfast was included, after which they could enjoy their free coffee out by the pool socializing with other guests. They could visit the motel restaurant for additional meals. What's not to love? For those not needing extensive medical care, this sounds like a truly workable option.

In a similar vein for the more adventurous is the cruise ship option. Those who go on repeated cruises with the same cruise line get excellent prices, and a four-month world cruise can cost significantly less than four months in assisted living. Ships have full-time medical staff on board (not so at some traditional facilities). The food is great, with a wide variety, and there are free entertainment options, including live musicals, magic shows, and lectures. And did I mention that you are waited on day and night? Frequent cruisers on the same ship may even have a permanent name placard on their cabin door.

One snag in this plan is the downtime of a day or two between cruises, but most permanent cruisers can stay with family or in a port hotel in the interim. The obvious benefit, beyond those listed, is that seniors get to visit all the "bucket list" locations they were too busy to see when they were younger.

Sometimes two or more elderly persons may live together, sharing the tasks that are too much for one person to bear alone and caring for each other during illnesses. Think "college roommates," only sixty to seventy years later. Dubbed "do-it-yourself senior living," this approach works well provided that at least one of the residents is slightly younger or more capable than the others and that personalities are compatible. Residents may share a home owned by one of them or purchase or lease a home together. There are all kinds of possibilities; examples abound of do-it-yourselfers living together in high-rise apartments, suburban neighborhoods, and RV parks.

While there can be downsides to very old seniors living together, it's a beautiful thing when people can grow old together and help one another. In their *New York Times* best seller, *Having Our Say*, sisters Sarah L. Delany and A. Elizabeth Delany detail their long, productive life together. To one another, they are Sadie and Bessie. Sadie was a noted educator and author, and Bessie was the second African American female dentist licensed in New York. The book opens with Sadie writing, "Bessie and I have been together since time began, or so it seems. Bessie is my little sister, only she's not so little. She's 101 years old, and I am 103." She goes on to say, "Neither one of us ever married and we've lived together most all of our lives, and probably know each other better than any two human beings on this Earth. After so long, we are in some ways like one person. She is my right arm. If she were to die first, I'm not sure if I would want to go on living because the reason I am living is to keep *her* living."[4] Bessie lived to be 104, dying nearly four years before Sadie. Sadie lived to be 109.

Just Come Live with Us

The simplest solution may be the one you begin with or the one you end up with, but it's not always the wisest. In the midst of all the unrest and confusion, it's tempting for caring adult children to say, "Mom, why don't you just come live with us?" Those who make this offer deserve extra stars in their crowns for returning to the multigenerational solution that worked so well in the past. But choosing this path today can be challenging.

Even families who can get through every Thanksgiving dinner and summer visit without coming to blows can be tested when the generations are living together permanently. Major adjustments like sleeping arrangements and even bathroom accommodations can be worked out more easily than daily issues like how high to set the thermostat, what to serve for dinner, where to set the TV volume, and how to discipline children. Over time, these and other minor issues can raise the stress level of everyone in the house to the breaking point.

Yet according to a study conducted by AARP, multigenerational households in the United States increased from 6.2 million in 2008 to 7 million in 2010.[5] While this doesn't mean we're returning to the days of the Waltons quite yet, it is a definite trend. The report states that the downturn in the economy during those years may explain the increase.

And it can work. After both of Julie's parents passed away, she and her husband decided to move Freda, her grandmother, from West Virginia into their home in Colorado. Freda shared a bedroom with Jessa, age twelve. Jessa not only didn't mind, she enjoyed having her great-grandmother with her.

Julie chronicled life with Grandma in her blog, *Fridays with Freda*. Freda taught Julie how to make the homemade vegetable soup she remembered as a girl, rinsed the dishes after every meal, and passed along wisdom like, "It's Good Friday, time to plant your potatoes." Freda went with the family on a back country Jeep ride with the top down but could opt in or out of family outings and ball games. Everything went extremely well—until it didn't.

As Freda became increasingly confused, mixing up generations and not remembering where Julie and her husband Jeff had gone when they left the house for work, the family decided it was time to move her into an assisted living community. But none of them, including Jacob, fifteen, would have missed the time they had Freda with them for anything. When the kids were told their great-grandmother would be moving out, they said, "But how will we see her every day?"

Julie says, "She had eighteen months with our family. While it was difficult some days, when she passes away I will know we were all given a special gift. Especially my children, who had never lived around grandparents before." That's the blessing of the multigenerational home.

Often, families who understand their situation with an aging parent is only for a season will put pencil to paper and realize it makes better sense to add a room with bath onto their existing home, or to finish a basement, than to spend all that money on assisted living. Once the elder passes, they are left with a more valuable home and a really neat pad for a teenage son or daughter to move into.

Laney's mother and dad both had significant heart issues and lived in a three-level house. "It was just too much for them and they didn't know what to do," Laney said. "My husband and I discussed it and decided that building onto our home was a great option for them." Her parents' apartment is attached to the family home by a doorway, so sometimes privacy is an issue. Still, now that Laney's dad has passed away, she says, "It's a blessing to me to know that I am here if Mother ever needs anything. She is comfortable and feels like she still has a home. I think that is a blessing for her too."

In China, a "stacked house" with one generation per floor is common. The eldest live on the bottom floor, and when they pass on, the next generation moves down. Not a bad idea.

In this country, families are more likely to build a separate guest house in their back yard for elderly parents—and it doesn't have to be too costly. Ken Dupin, a minister in Salem, Virginia, developed so-called MedCottages with help from Virginia Tech researchers after studying family-managed care in other countries. A MedCottage, also called a "granny pod" by some, costs about $85,000 (roughly a year or two in assisted living) and has a twelve-foot by twenty-four-foot living area with a handicapped-accessible bathroom, kitchen, and hospital bed. It's wired so the person living there can be monitored twenty-four hours a day—a perfect combination of independence and safe family care. These cottages also make great guest quarters later. The only caution is, be sure to check zoning regulations and building requirements in your area before placing your order.[6]

When deciding on the right solution for an aging parent, we may wish we were clairvoyant. How long will mom or dad live? Sometimes a terminal diagnosis indicates how long this season will last, but most of us go into it clueless. Had we known that my mother-in-law would live less than four months after moving into assisted living, we would have convinced her to come stay with us. The guest room on our main level could have accommodated her. The bathroom nearby could have been adapted for her use, and we could have had home health care to help with her hygiene.

But we didn't know. Had it been four years instead of four months, it would have taken a considerable toll on our home life and perhaps on our relationship with her. During this same time, my sisters and I received some helpful advice regarding our mother's care: if you can afford outside help, take it. That way you can continue to be your mother's daughter, not her hands-on caregiver. That advice influenced our thinking about my mother-in-law, too.

Besides, like many elders used to living independently, Mary Frances didn't want to be a bother. So instead of coming into a home she had visited regularly and where she would be loved and welcomed, she moved into an assisted living center. We spent a lot of time and money fixing up her studio apartment to make it homey for her. Still, I remember the afternoon I dropped by and she commented offhandedly, "I just can't believe I'm going to live here the rest of my life." I resisted the urge to placate her with platitudes and simply said, "I know it must be hard." It is hard, but once the decision is made it can get easier.

My mother was in the same apartment in her assisted living community for five and a half years. She wasn't happy about moving there at first. But almost one year to the day after she moved in, during one of my regular visits, she asked to take me and my two sisters to lunch.

Excitedly, she gave each of us a gift: a beautiful, porcelain pansy blossom that I still have. "You girls made the right decision for me," she said. "Thank you. I'm sorry I made it so hard on you." It was a good thing we each had a napkin in our laps, because our tears of relief were plentiful.

Toward the end of my mother's life, when she was hospitalized from the effects of breast cancer and congestive heart failure, her longtime doctor and friend presented her with the option of hospice care. She said she thought that would be a good idea. Then she said, "I just want to go home." Home to her, at that moment, was her apartment in assisted living.

You can get through this season. I promise. But don't believe me. Trust in the goodness of God. The psalmist cried out in Psalm 71:9, "Do not cast me away when I am old; do not forsake me when my strength is gone." Rest assured, God knows what you are going through. He listens, and He definitely does not intend to cast away or forsake your loved one. So once you've cried the tears, prayed the prayers, and made the best decision you can for the elders you love, it's time to transform their new residence—wherever it is—into a home.

Chapter 4

PUTTING THE HEART
IN HOME

Lord, you have been our dwelling place
throughout all generations.

—Psalm 90:1

My heart skipped a beat when I saw on the caller ID that my mom was calling from her assisted living apartment. She was in Tennessee and I was in Colorado. This is a woman who never made long-distance calls lightly. If she did call, she had a list of everything she wanted to say right by the phone—and the person on the other end of the line had little chance of deterring her from moving from one item to the next. I often thought I could say, "Mom, I think I'm having a heart attack. I have to go," and she'd reply, "Oh, I see. Well, the next thing I wanted to tell you is . . ."

So when I saw she was calling, I was apprehensive. But this time she was a woman on a mission.

"Do you remember that little plaque you had in your kitchen when you lived in Germany with the military?" she asked as soon as I said hello. "The one that said, 'Bloom Where You Are Planted'? I want you to send that to me. Some ladies here need to read it."

I did remember the plaque, I just didn't know if I still had it. I'd moved five times since then. What were the odds I'd find it in one of those neglected boxes in the storage room? But I did! By some miracle, it had survived all the culling and I was able to get it right in the mail to my mom.

My mom wasn't always so comfortable at her assisted living community or such an encouragement to others. Chances are good your older loved ones won't exactly embrace the idea of giving up their home and moving into a strange new place either. To understand their reticence, all we have to do is project twenty or so years to when we will be in the same situation. How will we react to being asked to leave the one place on earth that feels like home? How easy will it be for us to sort through a lifetime of accumulated stuff and watch most of it be carted out to the trash or donation bin? The process can be agonizing for everyone involved. Fortunately, there are helpful guidelines we can follow or at least consider.

Before the Move

There's an optimal way to get things accomplished—and then there's the way they eventually get done. Before I share my accumulated wisdom about how to begin moving an elder adult into a care facility, let me acknowledge that just as living arrangements can be as different as the persons we are trying to help, so too the process of the move.

My older sister often likened my mother's move to assisted living to a vacation from which she simply never returned. Emotionally, after living in one house her whole adult life, this was the only way my mother could cope with the change. She had been living with my sister for weeks, so she had packed some basics. But she never went back to the house to decide what to take. My sisters made all those decisions. Once they had a lovely apartment prepared for Mom, I flew into town to help with final touches, we took her to the apartment, and she moved right in. What made this "permanent vacation" technique plausible, however, was the fact that her lifelong home was mortgage-free and we could comfortably promise that everything would stay the way it was for at least six months. Although Mom went by the house for a pair of earrings or shoes she wanted for a certain outfit, once she agreed to our joint decision for her to move to assisted living, she never looked back.

That's one approach, but it's not the one experts recommend. Most advise a prolonged period of getting ready for the move, thus giving your loved one time to adjust to the change slowly. Suggested steps for downsizing the present living location include the following.

Designate assets. Hopefully your parent or loved one has already designated items they wish to pass down to family members or to others they know. If not, this is the first step—and one to be handled with the greatest amount of tact and sensitivity. Once items are identified and tagged, ask recipients to come and collect them if possible.

Safeguard keepsakes. Everyone knows not to toss out diamond rings and photo albums, but what about the less obvious keepsakes? After my mother-in-law passed away, one granddaughter was thrilled to find a rusty old jar of cinnamon sugar, the only treasure she really wanted, still in the kitchen cupboard. Why her delight? Because she remembered summer visits when her grandma fixed cinnamon toast for her each morning. Any rational "sorter" would toss something like that on the first pass, and certainly any professional service would also. When in doubt, ask. And set aside a place for special keepsakes.

Establish a timeline. If the move is precipitated by a health crisis, then everything may have to be accomplished at lightning speed. Assuming that's not the case, experts advise dedicating a few hours a day to the task of sorting and cleaning out a primary residence rather than a weekend marathon. The slow-but-steady approach makes it less likely that treasures will go out with the trash, and it's easier on everyone's emotions. Establishing a moving date and working back from there helps determine what to do when.

Set up a system. Think about the process you go through when you clean out your closet seasonally, and then expand the concept. Setting up places in each room for the following categories helps tremendously: keep, pass on, donate, and toss. When elders are working with you, it can be helpful to include a fifth category: decide later. Just don't let this pile outgrow the others. Start with the least-used rooms in order to protect your elders from clutter and disruption of daily life for as long as possible.

Expect emotions. I volunteered to spend one morning a week helping my mother-in-law go through her closets and cupboards. After just two successive weeks, she declared, "I don't want to do this anymore. You can do it when I'm gone." We stopped, and although she later said she enjoyed the extra space our efforts created, she never wanted to resume the process. I think it was just too emotional for her. It can be hard to be reminded of a time of life when you wore a certain dress or baked a favorite birthday cake for a beloved husband long gone. Yet some of the emotions evoked as you sort will be cathartic, and on the best days, some will have you rolling on the floor laughing together. Just be aware of emotions—yours and those of your elder—and proceed accordingly.

Record stories. If you're blessed to be going through the downsizing process with your parents, be aware of the stories that will emerge in the process and take notes or record impromptu conversations. Maybe your dad says, "This is the hammer I had when I started the construction business," then goes on to tell of the challenges of being a small business owner. Maybe your mom says, "I wore this hat to my mother's funeral. Did I ever tell you about the time she and I took a road trip to Florida?" Whatever thoughts or memories are unearthed, they are worth keeping in the "save" pile.

Hire professionals. This is often the last option for a reason. An objective approach to a house full of accumulated living may be efficient and practical, but it puts all the sentimental items and keepsakes at risk. If you live far away and have no siblings to help, this may be your only option, and there are good services available. (Check local listings or visit the National Association of Senior Move Managers, www.nasmm.org, to learn more.) If you make this choice, please take the time to do an inventory, perhaps marking valuables and keepsakes with colored stickers, in advance of handing a stranger the key.

Finally, as difficult as it may be on some days, try to keep the whole process as positive as possible. If your elders have always been philanthropists in their community, remind them that people will appreciate using the items they are giving away. Keep the colorful brochures from the place they are moving to in plain sight, and continue to remind them of the benefits of moving to a place with fewer maintenance problems and greater safety—or whatever your elders' primary motivators are. If they find it hard to part with certain things which would be impractical for the new residence, offer to store them (at least temporarily) at your house. You may have to sacrifice some much-needed storage space, but making room for your dad's toolbox or your mom's sewing machine can bring great peace of mind. Laugh and hug as much as possible.

It's Moving Day

The day my sisters and I took my mom to her assisted living apartment, we kept sensing we'd experienced it all before. This made no sense until one sister exclaimed, "I know what it is—it's just like drop-ping a kid off at camp!" I don't want to seem disrespectful to the aging in the least; however, the similarities are remarkable.

Seeing an attractive woman seated in the hallway, we steered our mom in that direction. "She looks nice, Mom. Why don't we go over and meet her? Maybe she plays bridge." How like the efforts parents make to ensure their children make new friends at camp.

Concerns and complaints about the food in the dining hall are also similar, as is the clothing situation. Since my mother-in-law was in assisted living in my hometown, I was the one charged with trying to keep up with all her laundry—a frustrating and fruitless endeavor. The only solution was to make sure her name was boldly imprinted on every single piece of clothing, sheet, pillowcase, and towel—just like at camp.

We expect our kids to participate in camp activities, and we hope our parents in assisted living will engage as well. In an effort to encourage my mom-in-law, I decided to join in one of the activities. Several times I called and reminded her that I was coming on Monday for the apple butter festival. When the day arrived, I entered her room with a cheerful, "Hi! I'm here for the festival. Are you ready to go?" She replied, "I'm not going to that. Why are you going?" In this, as in many aspects of caring for our elders, it helps to keep a sense of humor.

But there are serious comparisons, too. We entrust our children to the care of camp counselors, but we can't help but wonder if our kids are all right in the middle of the night. How often I woke up won-dering if my mother and mother-in-law were truly safe. Was someone sneaking into their rooms to rob them of the few personal possessions they still had? What if they had fallen out of bed and were unable to call for help? At such times, whether with kids at camp or moms in assisted living, the best thing we can do is pray. In both cases, we send them off with our best intentions—and a whole lot of faith.

Once the decisions are made, the funds are secured, the sorting is over, and the new residence is prepared, you arrive at moving day—and rarely will you experience a day more packed with both anticipation and anxiety. Yes, it's a fresh beginning, full of hope. But will your mom like it? Will your dad make friends? Will they even agree to stay there? And there's the unspeakable question that still haunts you with every box you carry in: Did we make the right decision?

Conventional wisdom dictates completing the move as expeditiously as possible. If you need to hire professional movers to take care of the heavier loads, do so. Coordinating this move may feel like a major military operation, but the planning will be worth it in the end. Begin using the facility to which your elder is moving as the resource it claims to be. How does the place recommend you orchestrate the move in order for it to go most smoothly? What time of day is best? Who on staff might be available to help?

As in all aspects of caring for elderly parents, asking others who have gone through such a move for their advice, their top dos and don'ts, can be extremely valuable. You are in uncharted territory. Ask other travelers for direction.

Once the mechanics of the move are completed, it's time to make the new residence feel as much like home as possible. Decisions made beforehand about location, sunlight, size, and so forth are all part of creating a pleasing, homey environment. As with most moves, though, it's when you add the decorative details that the real transformation takes place.

Almost Like Home

In our imaginations, our parents handle a move to an assisted living facility or long-term care facility just as they handled other moves in their lives. We imagine our mom carefully selecting the furnishings she wants to move from her home and then standing in the middle of the new living environment, directing movers and family members where to put what. I suppose this has happened someplace, somewhere—just not in my experience.

My mom was a willing nonparticipant in setting up her new assisted living apartment. My sisters started the process by taking her around to visit different locations, finally getting her to the place where she conceded, "Well, if I have to choose a place, I guess I'd pick this one." Then they went to work selecting the best of the available apartments, having the walls painted Mom's favorite color of yellow (not always allowed; ask first), and blending selected items from our family home with new, traditional-style furniture chosen to fit well into the space.

The result was a lovely, cheerful environment that became a show-case where the facility's managers brought prospective residents. Mom served as a gracious greeter and hostess, a role she naturally embraced.

By the time I got to town almost everything was done. I loved what my sisters had selected from Mom's home. They had even brought the little secretary desk my dad gave Mom when she was elected president of the library board to use for her personal business and correspondence. The bedroom featured a bright yellow and gold floral comforter, and Mom's framed needlepoint works were on the wall. I was able to add finishing touches like a pansy bathmat, pansy key rack (yes, she loved pansies!), and a small shelf to showcase the collection of tiny designer shoes I had been sending my mom for birthdays and Mother's Days. When every last thing was in place, down to stocking the small refrigerator with her favorite beverages, we brought Mom over.

After all the heartache of the weeks leading up to this day, we weren't sure what to expect. But my mother graciously calmed our anxieties by exclaiming over and over how much she loved every-thing—running her hand over the silky tapestry of her new gold couch and sitting on the edge of the bed to test her new mattress. It was like the "reveal" on a home makeover show! Her "welcome party" was a huge success, with the community's manager and activities director stopping in to welcome her.

Inevitably, though, it came time for us to go and for Mom to stay.

My sisters had homes and husbands to tend to, priorities my mother always honored. But since I was visiting from out of town, she turned to me and asked, "Would you stay with me—just for tonight?" Of course I said yes.

After a nice dinner in the dining room, where Mom met a few of the residents, we got into our nightgowns, robes, and slippers and settled in to watch TV in her new home. Suddenly a loud announcement made us both jump. "Residents, we will be showing our featured movie, *Grumpy Old Men*, in the activities lounge in just a few minutes. Come on down."

My mother turned to me. I wondered what her reaction would be. "Well," she said, "I certainly didn't come all the way here to look at grumpy old men." Our laughter, added to all the love my sisters and I had already poured into her new living environment, was the final touch needed to make this strange new place feel like home.

Creating an assisted living apartment for my mother-in-law was both a similar and a different experience. Because of her macular degeneration, we were advised to consider a smaller, studio-style apartment; that way, she would find it easier to learn her way around. Only one small chest of drawers, a favorite recliner, a few family photos, and a floor lamp made the move from her home in Pueblo, Colorado, to assisted living in Colorado Springs, where my husband and I live. We purchased a twin bed and mattress and a small dining table with two chairs to complete the furnishings, and I set to work adding the designer touches.

As I was strolling through Bed, Bath & Beyond, a display of bedding and towels in a bright Southwest pattern caught my attention. This was just what we needed. My mother-in-law was born and lived her whole life in Colorado. Muted, toned-down, neutral colors were not for her. This was a woman with a turquoise and chrome kitchen—a woman who very reluctantly gave up the turquoise and green shag carpeting upstairs, and the orange shag carpeting downstairs, when her home needed to be re-carpeted for her own safety. The tapestry pattern of deep red, orange, and turquoise was perfect for her—so we splurged on the bedding, throw pillows, and coordinating towels.

Four months later, after she had passed away and we were giving away or selling the contents of her apartment, I momentarily questioned the wisdom of spending so much on her new decor, but I'm still glad we did. On one of my visits after Mary Frances moved in, she said, "Everyone who comes into my room tells me how pretty it is. I really can't see it well, but thank you." My pleasure. Truly.

Do you catch the common theme in these two stories? The overriding goal of anyone wanting to help older adults transition into a new stage of life should be the preservation of, and respect for, who they are—not only their personal identities but their personal preferences as well. If you make that your number one design principle when helping to set up their new residence, you can't go wrong. Not only will they be more at home in their new environment, but the furnishings will (we hope) also remind the aides and workers that these are people of substance and worth—people with rich and full lives to remember; people to celebrate and value.

I've been in and out of many assisted living apartments in my years of volunteering. The differences are dramatic. Some abodes are so comfy, inviting, and homey that you want to linger—maybe put the kettle on for a spot of tea if the room contains a stove. Others are institutional and stark. One room I enter has only a twin bed with basic bedding and a row of oxygen tanks. I don't know the backstory; maybe it has to do with allergies to fabrics. But the woman who lives in this room is not this one-dimensional, and her home should more accurately reflect who she is. My family was blessed with funds to spend, but it need not cost a lot to give a room personality and warmth.

In the best of situations, the apartment or room is furnished with a bedroom suite, comfy chairs, lamps, and artwork that were all previously selected by the resident and reflect his or her lifelong preferences.

These furnishings often have a story attached: "the lamp we bought when we were stationed in Japan"; "the quilt my mother made for me when we got married." Stuff is just stuff—we all know that. But when you can be surrounded by some of your *own* stuff, you feel more at home.

A common element in these more personally furnished apartments is a photo of a deceased spouse, prominently displayed. Or maybe it's the couple's wedding portrait, still in the first frame they put it in. My mom and a lifelong male friend became special companions in their later years, after both their spouses passed away. My sisters and I knew Cecil our whole lives and loved him dearly. His photo was in my mom's living room. But only my dad's photo was in her bedroom. A bit confusing for some visitors, but not for us.

Collections of reasonably sized items make wonderful additions too. Just pray your mom collects thimbles or figurines and not old typewriters (a collection I started but had to abandon for practical reasons). My mom filled a small glass-front curio cabinet with items that served as props for the stories she liked to tell inquiring visitors. Inside was a place setting of her wedding china, a few pieces of her silver flatware (used to entertain at holidays and parties hundreds of times over), and an artist's rendering of our family home where she spent the majority of her adult life. Awards she had won in her lifetime were also on display, giving visitors a chance to learn what causes and organizations mattered most to her. This curio cabinet was the first stop on the apartment tour my mother relished giving to visitors.

The first hint about who lives inside an assisted living apartment or long-term care room is often displayed near or on the outside door. We made sure my mom had seasonal wreaths, and a little built-in shelf right next to the door showcased other decorative items she loved. In the fall, her entryway was always decorated in the orange and white colors of the University of Tennessee. No one entering that apartment would have any question as to which team she supported!

What to Wear?

While not a part of setting up the new residence per se, your older parent's wardrobe deserves some careful forethought. This isn't the time to ask a woman who has dressed stylishly all her life to live out the rest of her days in housecoats, but practicality and comfort certainly merit consideration.

My older sister knew the style of clothing my mom had gravitated toward in her later years, and she filled Mom's closet with new elastic-waist pants and colorful blouses that were easy to put on and care for. Still, my mom kept some of her nicer outfits from home for special occasions—and all her costume jewelry.

As vain as it sounds, my mother considered putting together a colorful, seasonal outfit with matching jewelry to be a personal ministry of sorts. "The ladies at my lunch table always like to see what I'm wearing," she said one day. One of my memories of her toward the end of her life was when she looked at me from the bed where she had been confined for several days and said, "I can't believe I'm never going to wear any of my cute outfits again." I offered to help her get dressed if she would like, but she thought about it and then said, "No, that's OK." I'm glad she made an effort to dress attractively for as long as she could, because it lifted her spirits and those of the other ladies.

Dressing attractively each day was a bigger challenge for my mother-in-law because of her sight problems. It was impossible for her to know if she had on navy blue or black slacks, for instance, and stains went unnoticed because she simply couldn't see them. One of my biggest frustrations was that the attendants who dressed her each morning seemed to put no thought into coordinating a nice outfit. When I entered the room, she would ask, "What am I wearing today? What color are these slacks?"

This was a woman who dressed impeccably most of her life. Mary Frances worked at her husband's business even after his death, and she always wore well-made suits, tweed blazers, and appropriate jewelry. She enjoyed buying an expensive outfit occasionally, and she kept track of what it cost her each time she wore it to make sure she got her money's worth out of it.

Knowing this, I did everything I could to make it easier for the aides to dress her in something that at least matched. I would pair a shirt and slacks on two hangers in her closet, leave a three-inch space on the rod, and then hang another matching outfit. Yet time and again I arrived to find her in mismatched clothing, the low being the day she had on competing plaids. No wonder she stopped going to the dining room for lunch and asked to be served in her apartment. Her pride of appearance was still intact, and she couldn't trust that she looked presentable.

Our primary concern for our older adults is that they be cared for physically. We want to know they are free of pain, safe, and warm. But we also want to do all we can to maintain their self-respect and sense of identity, and dressing as closely as possible to how they always have is an important factor.

One word of caution: even in the nicest of facilities, items can mysteriously disappear from residents' rooms. It's heartbreaking for the older adult when this happens, because anything that has survived so much downsizing is often valuable to them, if only for sentimental reasons.

If something is a family heirloom or of great monetary value, it may be best to keep it elsewhere and take your aging parent to visit it regularly. As for jewelry, the most expensive pieces should either be worn at all times or secured in a safe in the front office, if possible. Or you could be the temporary custodian of your mom's nicest jewelry, bringing it to her whenever you go to pick her up for a special occasion. She will welcome your help with the clasps anyway, and you can admire the final effect together.

Chapter 5

❧

DRIVING OR NOT?

I am the LORD your God, who teaches you what is best for
you, who directs you in the way you should go.

—Isaiah 48:17

My mother waited in the car while I ran into a grocery store to pick up a few things she needed. When I slid back into the driver's seat next to her, she was pointing her finger insistently toward the far side of the parking lot.

"See that old couple over there?" she asked. "I know I can drive better than they can."

I looked across the lot to see an elderly woman, grocery bag in each hand, slowly moving toward her parked car. As she walked, she rocked from side to side, a pretty good sign both knees were bad. About ten feet behind her was an elderly gentleman with a walker, shuffling along to keep up as best he could.

"Mom," I said, "we are going to get out of here before we find out how well they can drive." We both laughed, and I was relieved that the subject of her driving had been successfully circumvented one more time. She had already agreed not to drive. I certainly didn't want to revisit that decision. I had seen the X-rays of her osteoarthritic knees, and they were pretty much bone on bone. For years she had said, "I can drive anywhere I want to. I just can't get out of the car after I arrive!" Not a good thing.

A story circulating on email describes an older woman driver who calls 911 to report that someone has stolen her steering wheel. When the officers arrive, they find her seated in the back seat of her car.

Another account tells of an older woman who hears on the news that a driver is going the wrong way on the interstate. She knows her husband often takes that route, and he's out running errands, so she calls his cell phone to warn him. "*One* person going the wrong way?" he exclaims. "Not just one. They all are!" Funny stories unless your parent is the subject.

Of all the talks we must have with our aging parents when they begin losing the ability to do everything they've always done, the talk about whether they should continue driving is one of—if not the— hardest of all.

When I asked my friend Gail what had been difficult for her in caring for her dad, she said, "Taking away my father's driver's license. My dad loved to drive. He had driven in his career as a mailman, and he loved long driving trips with his family. After I took him to a driving assessment center and they told him he could not drive, he cried. I had only seen my dad cry two other times in my life: when my sister died at sixteen and when my mother died after their fifty-two years of marriage. The loss of his license symbolized his loss of independence."

In her book *Caring for Yourself While Caring for Your Aging Parents*, author Claire Berman shares a similar father-daughter conversation between a woman named Georgina and her dad, but with a different outcome.

"Daddy had a car wreck a month ago," she explains. "He ran into two other people, and he almost killed himself. Since he lives out in the country, far from any form of public transportation, I looked into ways that would make it possible for him to manage without a car. I found out which stores would deliver, gave him the names of transportation services, and even located a student who would drive my father on errands for a small fee. Daddy said, 'Thank you so much,' and then went out and bought a new car. That's pretty typical of our relationship. I do the research and make suggestions. He does what he wants."[1]

Generally speaking, it's more difficult for a man to admit that he shouldn't drive than it is for a woman, although it can be gut-wrenching for both. In her book *A Bittersweet Season*, author Jane Gross wrote: "My anecdotal observation is that men are more stubborn about driving than women, just as women are more stubborn about leaving their homes. So in this particularly difficult moment of role reversal, frequently the first of many, adult children are often facing down their father."[2]

When a couple is aging together, families report that an elaborate system of cover-up often develops. The husband may continue to drive, but his wife rides shotgun and tells him when to stop, when to signal, where to turn, etc. While it's understandable that a wife would want to be a helper-completer in this way, the dangers are obvious.

Even peers can be in on the scheme to protect a senior's right to drive. Whenever our friend Bruce arrived at the assisted living facility where his stepfather, John, lived, he was accosted by friends of his stepfather, also residents, imploring him not to take John's license away. "He's the only one who can still make runs to the liquor store for us," they petitioned.

When my mother-in-law moved into the same facility, Bruce warned us to avoid parking next to the big white Buick Century with the dings all over it, because that was John's car. Chances were he just might ding our car too. John couldn't turn his head to the right but didn't see that as a problem since Bruce's mom, Mary, could tell him what was on that side. Eventually John had to give up his license, but he, his wife, and his friends worked to preserve his driving for as long as possible.

Slowing Down

The change from independently driving yourself wherever you want to go to not driving at all is a huge one. If the facts allow and there hasn't been a game-changing accident, a gradual decrease in driving is preferable and gives the older adult a chance to get used to the idea of not driving. Wise adult children begin discussing the idea of life after driving long before it's necessary to take a stand. The following suggestions may help you broach the subject:

- Consider opening the discussion with a general question such as, "What if something happened and you couldn't drive anymore? What would you do?" What-if questions are less threatening and encourage advance planning.
- Use every opportunity to discuss the topic well before the need arises for an elder to stop driving. If your loved one comments about vision or hearing problems, for example, ask, "Do you think that could be affecting your driving?"
- Likewise, if there is an item in the newspaper or on a news broadcast about an elderly driver who confuses the brake with the gas pedal and crashes through a convenience store (which seems to happen with amazing frequency) or injures someone in an accident, simply say, "I'm so glad nothing like that has happened to you. What are you doing to prevent it?"

Often a gradual withdrawal from driving stems from physical limitations. Certain changes in vision related to aging make it harder to see at night, for instance, so often this is the first thing elders relinquish. (By the way, I've never known an elderly adult to turn down the offer of a ride when offered, so offer.) Suggest defensive driving strategies such as avoiding peak traffic times and major roads. Discourage driving in bad weather.

AARP sponsors 55 ALIVE, a low-cost driving refresher course, and AAA has an excellent, comprehensive self-rating test for drivers age fifty-five-plus. Taking one of these classes or assessments may put both the older driver and his or her family at ease, or it may reveal the extent of the problem with continuing to drive.

Older drivers (and I know many of us chafe at the definition of "older" as fifty-five-plus) can be helped to drive safely longer with a few minor adjustments and precautions. The AAA brochure "How to Help an Older Driver" lists several helpful suggestions:

- Schedule regular checkups and eye exams.
- Encourage regular exercise.
- Suggest a refresher course.
- Agree on safe limits.
- Choose the right car.

AAA recommends a car with height-adjustable seats; a tilt/telescoping steering wheel; height-adjustable safety belt anchors; good visibility; legible instruments; big, glare-proof mirrors; and convenience features such as power windows and locks.[3]

Often older drivers come up with their own adaptations in order to stay in the driver's seat longer. My mother-in-law would say, "It's OK. I only drive where I know where I'm going." One elderly woman gave up driving everywhere except to the end of her driveway to get the mail. Interesting that as teenagers we start out being allowed to drive only in the driveway, and some of us may end our driving careers in like fashion.

Jane Gross points out another interesting correlation between beginning drivers and seasoned ones. "In certain places, teenagers, as they grow into the driving experience, can obtain restricted or graduated licenses," she writes. "That would be a promising approach for the elderly. . . . In British Columbia, where there are daylight-only and maximum speed limits for older people, researchers recently reported in *Gerontologist* that there was an 87 percent reduction in accidents among those sixty-six and older between 1999 and 2006."[4]

I'm sure most Baby Boomers would vote for a graduated, restricted driver's license for seniors—until we have to apply for one ourselves. Whether those steps are approved by our states is probably up to us. And we can be a stubborn lot. We learned it from our parents.

To be fair, it isn't a given that we all have to give up driving as we age. Some people are able to continue driving well up into their years, and apparently without disaster. Bob Edwards, a Ngataki, New Zealand, man, was born before the first Model T was created. The oldest licensed driver in his country, he is still on the road at the wheel of a red, four-wheel drive Mitsubishi. He has been driving for eighty-eight of his one hundred five years and has no plans to give it up. After all, Edwards said, someone has to get groceries for his wife, who's ninety-one. He has been in just one crash and has just one speeding ticket. "I don't think I'm old," he said. "Not really."[5] Bob is definitely the exception.

Applying the Brakes

Just as it's often a fall that precedes a move into an assisted living facility, it may be a traffic accident that precedes the decision for an elderly adult to cease driving. Obviously we would hope to have the discussion and make the decision prior to an accident happening, but for logistical and emotional reasons, that doesn't always happen. We can only pray that the accident is a minor one if it does occur.

My sister-in-law Mary was more than shocked the day she got a call while at her nursing post in Colorado that her mom, who lived in Georgia, had driven her car up an electrical guide wire and was marooned there. Fortunately, emergency personnel were able to get her mom down uninjured, but her driving days were over.

When my mom had a traffic accident, she began every account of it with, "It wasn't my fault, but . . ." The accident wasn't technically her fault, and any driver can be involved in a traffic accident, but it was an indication that her reaction time might not be what it once was. Experts agree this is one of several signs it may be time to hang up the car keys.

Most reasons experts give for encouraging elders to cease driving are common sense. Unfortunately, hindsight is twenty/twenty, and a decision may be delayed because no one but the driver knows everything that happens, and he or she may be in denial about declining abilities. After an accident, siblings often begin to compare notes and realize their parent has been covering up his or her driving inadequacies for some time, perhaps not wanting to raise the question about safe driving or to be an additional burden on the family.

Studies show that "older drivers, especially after age 75, have a higher risk of being involved in a collision for every mile they drive. The rate of risk is nearly equal to the risk of younger drivers age 16 to 24. The rate of fatalities increases slightly after age 65 and significantly after age 75."[6]

To gather factual, objective data on the driving skills of an older person, it's helpful for someone to ride along and observe, jotting down notes if gathering empirical data seems useful. If riding along isn't possible, some adult children have followed their aging parent in their own car in order to observe driving ability. Besides an accident, what are the warning signs of driving impairment? Common ones include, but are not limited to, backing out of the driveway into traffic, riding the brake, incorrect signaling, hitting curbs, making dangerous lane changes, having difficulty merging onto a busy highway, failing to stop at stop signs or lights, and having trouble navigating turns.

I became most concerned about my mother's driving the day she came to a full stop on a four-lane highway and began backing up because she had missed her exit. She didn't see anything wrong with her corrective solution and certainly didn't see the need for me to brace myself and scream.

My sisters weren't as concerned as I was about my mother's driving early on. They lived in the same town as my mother and rarely needed to ride with her—and, I might add, they weren't in the car that day. I completely understood their reticence to take away our mom's independence, especially when it meant even more of their personal time would be devoted to her care in providing transportation. Still, I couldn't in good conscience neglect reporting my shocking experience.

Occasionally the facts speak for themselves. Adult children of older drivers need to get into the habit of scanning their parents' cars for additional dings, dents, and scrapes. And once a ticket is issued for driving too fast (or more likely, too slow) or for a traffic altercation in which their parent is at fault, it's time to discuss safe driving.

We had the law on our side when it was time for my mother-in-law to give up her license. Mary Frances and I had gone on a trip back East to visit family when the neighbor who was picking up her mail called my husband to tell him, "Some police officer keeps leaving his card on your mother's front door, and today he left a note saying that if she doesn't call him soon there will be a warrant issued for her arrest."

My husband immediately called the number on the card to speak with the officer. It turned out that the day before she left town, Mary Frances had sideswiped a parked car while on one of her errands. Someone had seen the accident and reported her license plate number to the police. She must have dozed off when it happened, however, because she truly knew nothing about it.

After Jim picked us up at the airport, we drove Mary Frances home. Jim told her about his conversation with the police officer and asked her if she remembered the incident. She didn't. "Let's go out in the garage and look at your car," he suggested. We went out and there it was: a long scrape running almost all the way down the right side of her two-tone blue sedan.

One thing that served my mother-in-law well as she aged was her pragmatism. Whether it was her failing eyesight or her deteriorating ability to drive, she was willing to accept the facts and learn to deal with them. To her unending credit and our great relief, her response to the accident, of which she had no recollection, was to give Jim her keys. Shortly thereafter, she sold her car.

"I could have really hurt someone," she stated. "I guess I have to stop driving now." We were all blessed that no one was hurt—and that she was so willing to face reality.

My mother, however, owned her champagne-colored sedan until the day she died. She didn't drive it for the last three or four years of her life, but it was parked outside the window of her assisted living apartment, just the other side of her bird feeder. She enjoyed watching both. The keys to the car hung on the key rack by her apartment door, but to our knowledge she never took herself for a spin after the day she said she wouldn't drive. She just loved knowing she could if she had to—or really wanted to.

I drove the car whenever I visited, and my sisters often took her places in it to keep it running smoothly. The manager of the assisted living community would occasionally call one of my sisters to ask if they would move Mom's car somewhere else since she wasn't driving it and parking was at a premium, but my sisters held firm. My mother was paying for a parking space, it made her happy to see her car parked outside her window, and there it was going to stay.

We were blessed that Mom agreed to stop driving as easily as she did. It wasn't a police officer who intervened this time but her trusted general practitioner. From conversations with my sisters, he already knew we were concerned about Mom's driving. After she was put on the blood thinner Coumadin for health reasons, her doctor said, "Now Lois, I don't want you driving while you're taking this."

There is no known medical correlation between that medication and the ability to drive (other than the risk of excessive bleeding in case of injury in a car accident), so this was a bit of a stretch. But my mother was from the generation of people who believe that doctors are second in authority only to God. So when the doctor took it upon himself to imply a side effect that wasn't there and told her not to drive, we were grateful.

If you would condemn us for relying on a white lie to keep the mother we loved out of the driver's seat, then you probably haven't gotten to this point in your parent's care. Desperate times call for desperate measures.

Experts concur that police officers and doctors are excellent professionals to talk with aging adults about driving safety. Grandchildren are also good candidates; often they can easily bridge the gap between their grandparents and themselves, leaping over that know-it-all generation in the middle. Trusted neighbors, friends, and caregivers might also be willing to broach this difficult and emotional subject. But if it's you who must initiate the conversation—and you'll know when it's time—there are tips with proven mileage to help you.

First of all, if there is a diagnosis of dementia, the concern may be greater but solutions may be easier. Doctors in most states are required to report dementia patients to the health department, and they in turn issue a report to the Department of Motor Vehicles. Often a medical report is required and a test will be given to determine whether the patient can still drive.

Aging expert Carol Bradley Bursack states that opinions vary on when people who've been diagnosed with dementia should quit driving. The Alzheimer's Association says that for some people, it's easier to give up driving earlier while they can still understand the danger of driving while impaired. Yet other sources say that people can drive safely during the early stages of Alzheimer's as long as they stay in familiar territory.

Carol's experience with her own father was heartbreaking. "My dad never had strong eyes and as he aged he naturally had more vision problems," she says. "After a close call where he could have had an accident, Dad voluntarily gave up driving. That was before he had surgery that left him with severe dementia. After dementia took over Dad's cognition, he went through many stretches where he angrily demanded that he could drive and that I was supposed to buy him a car. He no longer remembered that he'd wisely given up driving at an earlier time because it was the right thing to do. There was no use in my pointing out that at this time he had trouble even using a walker, and he couldn't see well enough to dial a telephone. He was sure he could drive and that was that. Those were heartbreaking times which we just had to weather until we could get him re-focused on some other issue."[7]

Before you discuss retiring from driving with older drivers, research transportation alternatives and present options. Make sure they understand that you respect their ability to make appropriate choices. Include times you can commit to providing transportation if possible. Offer to take the bus or taxi with them until they feel comfortable going it alone.

Personal transportation services for the elderly, both nonprofit and for-profit, are available in many communities. The SilverRide program in San Francisco, for instance, pairs willing drivers with seniors for a fee, but the drivers are more than chauffeurs; they are also companions. Drivers may take a client to run errands, and then they'll have lunch together. Or a driver will pick up one friend at a senior community, another at a private home, and the three will go see a movie. "We enable clients to have meaningful experiences outside the home and continue to lead normal lives," says cofounder Jeff Malz.[8]

Katherine Freund founded the Independent Transportation Network (www.ITNAmerica.org) after her young son (since recovered) was hit by an elderly driver. Now more than twenty-five communities in the United States have ITN affiliates. One part of the program allows seniors to trade their own cars for "points" they can later spend for rides, and enables volunteer drivers to also store transportation credits for their own needs.

My friend Pat said her mother became very comfortable taking a cab whenever she couldn't hitch a ride to church or bridge with a friend. Pat's mom became particularly fond of one male driver, so much so that she began to think of the older gentleman as her friend, and would change her plans if she couldn't get him at the time she wanted him.

When you begin your discussion, consider using "I" messages, which are always less accusatory: "I won't be able to sleep knowing you are on the road." Or, "I would never forgive myself if something happened while you were driving, and I never told you it was time to stop." Most parents don't want to cause their adult children extra anxiety. It's OK to play off that emotion to advance your position.

As a last resort, some adult children have arranged for their parents' cars to be towed or "booted," or they have disabled the cars mechanically. This seems like an extreme and disrespectful way to proceed, and it may only last until the parent gets the car returned or repaired, but it does send the message that this is a serious issue that can't be ignored any longer.

Once you feel you absolutely must ask a parent to make a responsible decision and stop driving, and you ask for the keys if he or she won't comply, do so with as much grace, respect, and gentleness as you can. As far as is possible, present the facts and your concerns, but let the decision be the driver's. Put yourself in his or her place.

If you are still uncertain whether this step is necessary, ask yourself this key question: Would I allow my kids or grandkids to ride in the car with this older driver? If the answer is no, then you must do everything you can to keep your aging loved one from driving, for his or her protection and the safety of everyone else on the road. Often just expressing your concern—that a grandchild you both love could be harmed—is more than enough. An unfit driver is a potential killer. There really isn't a nicer way to state that truth.

რ

FOCUSING ON FRIENDSHIP

A friend loves at all times.

—Proverbs 17:17

Old memories last longest, and musical memories seem to have the greatest staying power of all. Some of the songs I learned as a Girl Scout in the late 1950s and early 1960s will surely be with me until the day I go to sing hosannas in heaven. When my troop and I sang, "Make new friends, but keep the old. One is silver and the other gold," we had no idea that advice would apply to our aging years. But it does.

Helping someone adjust to the aging process is a constant effort to preserve as much as possible of what they loved about their younger years while helping that person adjust to the inevitable changes and losses that come with aging. Certainly anything adult children can do to help older parents keep up with friends who are still alive and to make new friends is time well spent. Sad to say, making new friends is important to replace the ones they lose.

Watching our grandmother turn to the obituaries in the morning paper while still sipping her first cup of coffee, my sisters and I used to think, "How morbid." Now I know it wasn't morbid at all. In her late eighties, she was losing good friends left and right, and she didn't want to miss the chance to say good-bye to someone—or send them off with a good hymn. My mother drove my grandmother to the funeral home time and again. She also drove her to visit friends and relatives who were still living. Mom saw those trips not as interruptions in her day but as the right thing to do.

Of all the gifts the Lord gives us, friendship is one of the best. When we are older and can reflect back over a lifetime, there are a few friends who stand out in our memories and our hearts. These are the people whose names and faces we will never forget. Even if they have passed on, we still remember their laugh, their smile, their caring touch, as if we were with them only yesterday. Losing such friends can be excruciating.

In her book *The Gift of Years*, Joan Chittister says, "For all of us the dying take a part of us into the grave with them—like conversations that can never be completed, dreams that can never be fulfilled. But for the elderly, the death of spouses, of loved ones, of friends, takes even more away—the memories, the sense of self, the feeling of community. If truth were known, too often the dead take the energy of the living, too."[1]

So how do we help the older adults we love deal with a loss of such magnitude? Certainly not by minimizing it or by refusing to talk about the person they grieve. When you visit, ask them about good friends they have lost. How did they meet? What did they like about one another? What would they change if they could? What do they miss the most about their friend?

Take the time to sit and look at old photos of lost spouses and friends with aging adults. Ask them to recount favorite experiences and memories. Reminding them that they have had successful, nurturing, relationships in the past can give them the courage to forge new ones.

"True, most seniors are healthy, alert, and totally functional," Chittister writes about friendship among the elderly. "But it requires effort and energy to make new friends now. And is it even worth the time? Friendship, after all, let alone love, takes a great deal of tending, a lot of talking, more getting-to-know-you time than we ourselves may have left. So why bother?

"The temptation to disengage is severe. And yet, our need for understanding, for comfort, for the sense of presence that comes with the voice at the other end of a phone call is greater than ever."[2]

Studies show that the existence of an intimate other is very important to satisfaction and psychological well-being in later life. Such intimacy helps prevent depression and anxiety. It gives security and significance to life. In the words of some older people themselves, it is "a port in the storm" and the "ultimate closeness against the night."[3]

The best we can do for the aging parents we love is to help them remember that friendship is a valuable part of life—one of the few areas of life they don't have to relinquish totally unless they decide to isolate themselves. It's well worth the effort to encourage them to engage.

Old Friends

The richness of a friendship that has spanned the decades is a treasure beyond description. Those caring for aging parents would be wise to remember the power and comfort of lifelong friendships and do all they can to help the elders they love sustain their key friendships, whether in reality or just in memory.

An old friend helps an elderly person maintain a sense of continuity. When friends who have known each other for decades look at each other's faces, they don't see an old person. They see each other as they were when they first met. A friend also makes an excellent audience for reminiscences and can supply the fun that's so important to a sense of well-being. And having a friend to confide in helps an older person cope more effectively with problems.[4]

"The Best Antiques Are Old Friends," reads a popular friendship saying. Whenever I see that motto stitched on a sampler or framed in a gift shop, I think of my mother-in-law, Mary Frances, and the friendship she shared for almost seventy years with Dorothea and Dorothea's sister, Jim (a nickname that stuck). All three of them are gone now, but while they were still alive, I had a chance to ask them how they became such good, lifelong friends.

"We met at the streetcar stop on Pearl Street in Denver when I was sixteen," Mary Frances remembered. "I lived in one apartment building, and Dorothea and Jim lived in the one next door."

"I saw her standing at the stop from my second story window," Dorothea recalled. "I knew she went to our school, so I decided Jim and I should go down and talk to her." The three were inseparable from that day on.

"One time we rode the streetcar together to a band concert at the park, but I couldn't even tell you who was playing," Dorothea said. "We talked a blue streak that night, and I guess we just never stopped."

One summer my husband and I took Mary Frances to New Mexico to Jim's eightieth birthday party. Although she was the youngest of the three friends, Alzheimer's was slowly robbing Jim of their shared memories. Through tear-filled eyes we watched Mary Frances and Jim embrace. Dorothea was there too, oxygen tank and all.

"If we live to be 103, we'll still be best friends, you and me," reads another friendship quote. How that speaks to the power and value of true friendship!

It's important for us to help our aging parents stay in touch with their friends who are still living. If old friends are nearby, offer to include them in family gatherings and provide transportation if necessary. Organize get-togethers such as a monthly card game. It will be easier to coordinate transportation if it's always at a set, prearranged time. Often friendships are forged through lifelong membership in the same VFW group, sorority, quilting circle, book group, or bowling league. As much as possible, help your parent stay in touch with the organizations that shaped who they are today. Maybe they can no longer make the weekly meetings, but can they make the annual Christmas party? Any way to keep them included is valuable.

When old friends are distant, encourage the elders you love to make regular phone calls, or place the call for them when you visit—then leave the room to give them privacy. (Your parent may need to vent about you!) Give them preaddressed, stamped envelopes and stationery so they can correspond with their friends easily. Too often our elders lose touch with old friends and relatives because they have all moved to be closer to children. This is where we can use our generation's technical savvy for good. Take the time to use online location services to get an updated address and/or phone number for your parent's close friends, and help them reunite.

The gift of friendship is too precious to discard along with all the other losses that can accompany growing older. We must encourage it in the elders we know and love.

Some of the dearest friends we will ever have in life can be siblings. My sister recently sent me a gift book full of silly sayings and soft sentiments about sisters. "Sisters . . . those people who you could disown one minute and passionately defend the next," one selection reads. "My sister and I are old now, but when I look at her, I still see the round faced little girl who shared double Popsicles with me, kept my secrets, and spent hours of days of a life just hanging out with me, enjoying being . . . related," reads another.[5]

Who could be a better friend than someone who has shared all the ups and downs of your entire life? Old rivalries and jealousies have a way of becoming far less important the older we get. It's more important knowing that someone else remembers how your dad sliced up watermelons on the picnic table in the back yard or the way your mom wiggled her backside when she stirred the gravy. Although we tend to remember details about family dynamics differently from our siblings at times, we all lived through the same events, and strong bonds are born of such common experiences.

Marion, a pastor's widow who played the piano beautifully, was extremely close to her twin sister. Separated in their later years by family obligations and circumstances, they now lived several states apart. Whenever I went to Marion's room at the assisted living community where I volunteer, Marion wanted to show me two things: the notebook of original poetry she intended to set to music one day and the letters she had received from her sister. Those letters were her most treasured possessions.

Often during our group Bible study, Marion would regal us all with a story from their shared childhood. "We loved to play church with all the neighborhood children," she would say, eyes sparkling. "There were some stone steps in the back yard, so my sister and I would make all the kids sit on those steps, and then we would hold church—reading from the Bible and singing hymns!" Marion suffered from dementia, so the older she got, the more often she told this story to us. Sometimes she told it several times within the hour we were together, but I never tired of hearing it— or of seeing her face light up as she remembered her sister, the fun they had, and the love that they still shared.

Often old friendships develop romantic overtones as people age. As I've mentioned, my mom had a late-in-life companion. Her best friend, Helen, was married to Cecil. My mom and dad and Helen and Cecil were couples-friends from junior high on. After Helen and my dad both passed away, Mom and Cecil kept being invited to the same gatherings. Eventually Cecil said, "There's no reason for both of us to drive. I'll swing by and pick you up." They were only in their mid-seventies at this point, so thus began a fifteen-year companionship that brought great joy to them both.

My sisters and I were very fond of Cecil. Our families had vacationed to Florida together many times over the years, so we already thought of him as a second dad. He was extremely witty, and we quickly welcomed him to family gatherings. We would not have minded one bit had Mom and Cecil decided to take the next step and get married, but they never did.

Still, the benefits of their relationship were many. They looked forward to seeing one another and having a reason to get dressed up. I'm sure they both ate more nutritiously than either would have without the other, as my mom would cook a real meal once or twice a week when Cecil came over—usually to watch a University of Tennessee ball game—and they had a standing date for brunch after church.

"We don't even have to tell each other entire jokes," Mom said on the day when she called to let me know what was going on with Cecil (lest I hear rumors of impropriety!). "We know all the same jokes, so one of us just remembers a punch line and we have a good laugh!"

New Friends

When my mom moved into assisted living, she told us, "I don't need to make friends with any of these old people here. I've had enough friends in my lifetime." But of course, being gregarious by nature, she did. She played bridge with the same ladies week after week, and they became very close to one another. When one of her bridge partners, Marge, passed away, she called to tell me. "I really loved her, you know," she said. We risk being hurt when we take a chance on friendship. But it's a chance worth taking.

It is said that friendship is a bridge between two hearts, so I suppose the question is whether we are willing to meet another person halfway across that bridge as we age or whether our bridges are more like drawbridges in the upright position. At any stage of life, we need friends. True friends can sense when one is feeling down without any words being spoken. Even when they are separated by miles, they often sense when one needs the other to get in touch. They are connected deeply.

Older adults living in community often find that the friends they make in that setting form a type of support group—similar to when a group of friends bands together to help one of their own survive breast cancer treatment or get through the loss of a loved one. This informal support group notices if you aren't feeling well at lunch. They save up funny stories to tell one another, and they celebrate together when someone gets a long-awaited phone call.

We develop close friendships when we are willing to spend time with other people. The more we get to know them, the more we trust them. The more we trust them, the closer we are to them. Within an assisted living community, we are often thrown together with people who may be dissimilar to us in terms of life experiences, education, ethnicity, even geographic histories. Yet those who are open to risk-ing new friendships can find connections within these communities. After all, older adults have more life experiences to share, and if they visit long enough, they are likely to find something or someone they have in common.

My friend Pat said that men were a rare commodity in the indepen-dent living community where her widowed mom lived in Maryland. So whenever the ladies gathered for bridge or a party, they would draft one of the few able-bodied men in the group to serve as host. In Pat's mom's apartment, a sign with the family name, Bagg, was hanging on the kitchen wall. "I used to work with someone named Tom Bagg at Diamond Labs during the war," the recruited host stated. "Oh," Pat's mom replied, "that was my husband." Needless to say, the two forged a strong friendship based on common acquaintances and memories.

My mom made another dear, late-in-life friend while in assisted liv-ing. It was her neighbor across the hall, Molly. Molly came over every night to tell my mom good night, and they would give one another a peck on the cheek and a hug. Touch is so important to older adults, so just that little bit of affection delivered in daily doses sustained them both. Sometimes Mom would invite Molly in for a beverage or to watch a favorite television show, and over time they simply grew to love one another and watch out for one another.

Molly also led a weekly Bible study with the residents, so she and Mom had the bond of faith as well. In that regard they had a mutual friend in Jesus Christ. Together they could praise Him for being the kind of friend who would never leave them or disappoint them. What a friend we have in Jesus!

Missy Buchanan is a writer, speaker, and friend to the aging. In her book, *Living with Purpose in a Worn-out Body*, she has included a beautiful essay on the value of late-in-life friends that you may want to share to encourage your elder to forge new friendships:

> These are not the friends who swapped campfire stories and ate s'mores with me. They are not the ones whose kids played hide-and-seek with mine on black-velvet nights. In fact, you won't discover them until the last few chapters of my life story. They are the late-in-life friends whose paths have criss-crossed with mine here at the senior center. They have their own stories, their own souvenirs, their own friends from the past. But all of us need late-in-life friends to come alongside as we complete the journey. O Lord, keep me from staying holed up in my room, using it as a self-imposed prison. Don't let me shut the door on new relationships. Nudge me to come out and be a late-in-life friend![6]

No adult child wants to be relegated to the role of matchmaker, scurrying around embarrassing our moms or dads by trying to make new friends for them, but there are some things we can do to encourage blossoming friendships. We can offer to include a new friend on a lunch outing or evening at the theater when we are hosting. We can stay for lunch and provide the conversational bridge to help elders connect with those seated at their table in the dining hall. To do this and more is to be a friend indeed.

Multigenerational Friendships

I can't remember whether I first met Myrtle in the professional organization to which we both belonged or because she was the special companion of my friend's dad. I only know we met and became fast friends. Myrtle was the same age as my mother, but I never saw her as a member of that generation. She was simply my timeless, beautiful friend. She loved me and I loved her.

I knew we were real friends the day Myrtle challenged me about a talk I had given at a local church. One she had attended. "You did a really good job," she said as we were walking from her downtown apartment building to a restaurant for lunch, "but you could do better." She was right: I could, and hopefully my talks now have more passion and intrinsic value because of Myrtle. Only real friends can challenge us to be our very best.

Everyone who knew Myrtle responded to her warmth and zest for life. She almost always wore a hat and wore it well. She claimed she was usually upgraded to first class when she traveled solely because of her hats. Myrtle and I traded notes about editors, publishers, and writing projects. One day she called me and said with a chuckle, "I just figured out I have to live to be 115 to get all my projects finished."

Myrtle had already accomplished so much. She had taught in universities around the world and published books on education. She enjoyed a long and happy marriage to a music educator, and they were quite a team till his death after their retirement. And she was in demand around town for her hilarious and heartwarming imitation of Julia Child!

I guess God decided Myrtle's life had been full enough, however. At eighty-seven, she was on a cruise when the symptoms of a brain tumor first showed. Told it was inoperable a few days after returning home, she accepted the diagnosis with grace and began setting her affairs in order. Those who loved her were blessed to have time to express their love and say good-bye.

One day when I was visiting Myrtle in the residential hospice where she spent her last days, I asked her, "Where is God in all this, Myrtle?"

"Oh," she said, "He's right here with me. When I close my eyes, I see the pages of my Bible rapidly turning. Then the flipping pages stop, and I see the book of John." She then quoted John 1:1–2 from memory: "In the beginning was the Word, and the Word was with God, and the Word was God." From that moment on, I had full assurance that I will see Myrtle again in heaven. Hopefully she'll have a productive writers' group organized for me to join.

I've been blessed to have other older friends in my life as well, several from the National League of American Pen Women, Pikes Peak Branch, to which Myrtle and I belonged. I'm also blessed to have younger friends. Women the ages of my daughters-in-law and stepdaughters, and younger, who seem to desire a real friendship with me. Rather than waste any time wondering why they want such an old friend, I've embraced the gift of their friendship. These young friends add life and fun to my days, and hopefully I can be a mentor to them in the Titus 2 model of older women teaching younger women what truly matters in God's eyes. Besides, I'll need someone to pick me up for night-time activities someday or visit me in assisted living.

I share all this not to brag about my ability to become friends with people of varying ages, but as a testimony to the beauty and value of multigenerational friendships. Friendships that go beyond superficial visits and small talk. Friendships that challenge, instruct, embolden, and nurture. Friendships no one is too old to experience.

So how can you encourage the parent you love to develop multi-generational friendships? Certainly pursuing a common interest, like writing or painting, is one way. Look for senior centers that encourage activities that blend different age groups. A daycare center in our town partnered with a senior center for extra help rocking babies and reading stories. It was a match made in heaven. The elders went home full of extra hugs and precious smiles, and the youngsters did, too.

Seniors from Cheyenne Place retirement home in Colorado Springs provide a similar service holding babies at Fort Carson's Army Community Services Nurturing Center. They cuddle and rock while parents are attending the Nurturing Parent class across the hall. "It's a win-win," said Jodi Dunn, activities director of Cheyenne Place. "The children give as much as we give to them."[7]

At the Grace Living Center in Jenks, Oklahoma, just outside of Tulsa, two classrooms were built into the facility when it was first built in 1998. Now sixty preschoolers and kindergarteners learn, play, and interact with the 170 residents. Their shared activities include reading to each other and acting out stories, and the setup has become a model for other facilities. "These kids are better readers because the grandmas and grandpas are there reading to them five days a week," says Grace's president, Don Greiner. The kids seem to think it's a good idea, too. According to kindergartener Liam, "We do activities, like trying new food. I tried a mint leaf and dark chocolate. I like school better with grandmas and grandpas."[8]

It is no doubt at church where the most multigenerational opportunities arise. A saintly woman at our church known lovingly as Grandma T recently went to be with the Lord at age ninety-seven. Her service was attended by people of all ages—and we laughed through our tears when we began to realize that we each thought we were her favorite! Grandma T was in the Word of God for eighty-seven years. She taught Sunday school most of that time and dispensed millions of hugs along with wisdom from the Lord. People who intersected with her at any stage of her long life were blessed. Her love spanned the generations.

When I was a single mother with two young boys, and living over a thousand miles from my closest relative, it was the church we attended that filled the multigenerational needs of my fractured family. I still remember fondly the older people who would pat my boys on the head and ask them how school was going—or remind them to mind their mother.

From the youngest babe in arms to the oldest attendee in a wheelchair, we are all part of the body of Christ. Our culture may have lost the benefits of several generations living together in one home, but the church can fill that void by bringing people of all ages together to worship and celebrate life. Do all you can to make sure the older person you love claims his or her rightful spot in the universal church family.

Hopefully our elders have in their hearts and lives a robust blend of old friends, new friends, and multigenerational friends. Friendships undergird their ability to age gracefully. Our prayer should be that, due to the richness of their friendships, they can echo the sentiments of that wise philosopher, Winnie-the-Pooh, who said, "If you live to be a hundred, I hope I live to be a hundred minus one day, so I never have to live without you."[9]

❧

Chapter 7

UNDERSTANDING THE AGING MIND

Set your minds on things above, not on earthly things.
—Colossians 3:2

I've observed that the difference between older adults who continue to live active, involved lives and those who seem content to sit and focus on their ailments is pure attitude. We are all going to experience episodes of forgetfulness, illnesses, aches, pains, perhaps even surgeries, broken bones, and joint replacements—and more of the above the longer we live. Our goal in helping the elders we love is to challenge them to focus on all they can still do rather than on what they have lost. We need to encourage seniors to keep their minds active and learning for as long as their bodies last.

The Brain

My husband and I like to work the crossword puzzles in the daily paper. In our paper, the puzzles are more challenging as the week progresses. We take turns working the Monday puzzle because that's the easiest. Either of us can usually complete the Tuesday puzzle as well, but by Wednesday we have to work together and pool our categories of knowledge to even have a shot at completing the puzzle. Never mind Thursday. We keep trying, however, because we know the brain is like a muscle that needs to be exercised in order to stay strong, and we want to stave off senility as long as possible.

Imagine our surprise, then, when we came across an article about Bernice Gordon, who recently turned one hundred and is still creating crossword puzzles for the *New York Times*. That's right: not working them, but *creating* them. "They make my life," she told a reporter. "I couldn't live without them." The *Times* didn't begin giving bylines to puzzle constructors until the 1990s, but it's believed they've been publishing Gordon's work since the 1950s. They've published more than 140 of her grids, and she's also been published in the *Philadelphia Inquirer* and in many crossword puzzle books. Gordon reports that she works best in the predawn hours in her home office in downtown Philadelphia, surrounded by two bookcases of dictionaries, almanacs, and other directories.[1]

From all we know about the aging brain, Bernice's ability to create puzzles at one hundred is based on one simple adage: use it or lose it. She never stopped using her brain, so it's still serving her well.

Still, medical research has compiled a warehouse of information on the decline of the aging brain. According to a special CNN report, research shows that as we cross the threshold into middle age, neural connections that receive, process, and transmit information can weaken from age and disuse. It may take us longer to learn new information. We often can't think as sharply or as quickly. Our reaction times may be slower.[2]

Researchers also tell us that older people in general have a harder time multitasking. We can become more forgetful, resulting in those tip-of-the-tongue moments where familiar words, names, and concepts lie just out of reach. An older person is more easily distracted and more prone to daydreaming and errors.

There are physical reasons why these changes occur. It's true: our brains are shrinking. The human brain normally can shrink up to 15 percent as it ages, a change linked to dementia, poor memory, and depression. Some surmise that our increase in longevity is the culprit, as the shrinkage can begin as early as age forty.

In addition, as the brain ages, it acquires the neural equivalent of sore knees and stiff fingers. Natural grooves in the brain widen. Healthy swellings subside. And tangles of damaged neurons become dense thickets of dysfunctional synapses.[3]

These facts aren't as dire as they sound. Not everyone's brain shrinks at the same rate, and even simple exercise like regular walking has been shown to curtail the deterioration. Stress and diet are significant factors too, so a low-stress, healthy lifestyle is not only the best way to stave off the physical effects of aging, but it can also have a dramatic positive effect on the aging brain.

We are all aging, and our brains are all changing one way or another. We can learn to cope with normal signs of decline by jotting reminder notes, entering key dates into smart phones, or muting the television when someone talks to us because we can no longer listen to two things simultaneously.

Yet we can also be our own worst enemies when it comes to aging. Again, it's back to attitude. A lecturer in a gerontology class I attended at the University of Colorado in Colorado Springs chastised the adults in the class for using the term "senior moment."

"I have college students in my classes who forget the paper they need to hand in or can't find their car keys," she said. "They are in their late teens and early twenties. So when you do the same thing, most likely it's because you have a lot on your mind, not because you are old. We need to stop expecting our minds to fail us. It's a self-fulfilling prophecy."[4] (By the way, another lecturer in the series was an eighty-year-old PhD who is still teaching ethics classes at the United States Air Force Academy—a prime example of active aging.)

Some of the changes in the aging brain are positive ones. "Whereas younger people may have better short-term and get-to-the-point-quick memory, older folks have had a greater variety of experiences and are better able to build a wider image out of a lot of different parts of memory," the CNN report continues. "They can make more connections because they have more things that have happened to them." In addition, the report shows, older people are better able to anticipate problems and reason things out than when they were younger.

More good news: "There are neuro-circuitry factors that can favor age in terms of innovation," observes Dr. Gary Small, professor of psychiatry and director of the UCLA Center on Aging. "The older brain is quite resilient and can be stimulated to innovate, create and contribute in extraordinary ways. We need incentives to encourage older people to continue to be creative because I think what they have to offer is tremendous."[5]

Does it sometimes take older people longer to retrieve information stored in their brains? Sure. But that's because they have so much more stored there—all tucked away in the folds of their neurons. They may not be able to find it when they want it, but it's still there. The brain is an organ, but like a muscle, the more we exercise our brains, the better they will perform. Crosswords and other puzzles are good; so is learning a foreign language or traveling to a new place. A change of environment stimulates the brain—one reason why some elders come alive with a move to assisted living, with all the activities and classes offered.

Learning to email or text grandkids is an excellent brain stimulator for many grandparents. At an assisted living community I visited, a Wii game was attached to the TV in the residents' lounge, and a grandpa was having a fabulous time playing the computer-generated games with his grandsons. Don't assume your elders aren't interested in learning something new. Introduce brain-exercising activities, or ask the grandkids to do so. You may be surprised at the response.

Most of us don't like the idea of brain shrinkage, but we truly can combat it through some of these activities, a healthy diet, and exercise. So normal aging in elders and in ourselves isn't really what we fear; rather, we fear the life-changing diagnosis of dementia, which may or may not include Alzheimer's disease.

Dementia

It is estimated that as many as 50 percent of elders over age eighty suffer from some degree of dementia, but it's important to understand the wide range of cognitive affliction and the importance of not labeling someone as demented prematurely. Mild cognitive impairment (MCI) is common as we age. People affected have memory problems, but not severe enough to be noticeable to other people or to interfere with daily life. There's no proof that MCI will eventually become dementia. But it could.

Dementia is generally described as a loss of mental function affecting a person's reasoning ability, memory, and thinking. It isn't usually recognized and diagnosed until the symptoms begin to seriously impair daily functions. Also important to note is that dementia is not a disease in itself, but rather a group of symptoms that may accompany certain conditions or diseases and may often result in changes in mood, behavior, or personality.

We hear more about Alzheimer's than other types of dementia, perhaps because this disease constitutes at least 60 percent of all dementia cases. But dementia also includes other less-common and less-talked-about forms. These include vascular dementia, Lewy body dementia, frontotemporal dementia, and Creutzfeldt-Jakob disease.[6] Parkinson's and Huntington's disease patients are also at risk for dementia.

Alzheimer's is defined as a progressive brain disease, resulting in the loss of brain cells. The condition is named after German psychiatrist Alois Alzheimer, who first identified it in 1906. The Alzheimer's

Association, the world leader in Alzheimer's research and support, has developed a checklist of common symptoms to help recognize the signs of Alzheimer's disease—what it is and what it isn't.

For example, difficulty having a conversation is a common sign of Alzheimer's or another form of dementia. Sometimes forgetting which word to use is not. Forgetting something and being unable to recall the information later could be dementia. Forgetting names or appointments temporarily is not. Also, people with Alzheimer's disease can become lost in their own neighborhoods, forget where they are and how they got there, and not know how to get back home. What's normal? Momentarily forgetting the day of the week or where you were going. (To see all ten warning signs of Alzheimer's disease, visit the Alzheimer's Association site at www.alz.org.)

Alzheimer's symptoms result from damage to the brain's nerve cells. The disease gradually gets worse as more cells are damaged and destroyed. Scientists do not yet know why brain cells malfunction and die, but the two prime suspects are abnormal microscopic structures called *plaques* and *tangles*. As the disease progresses and more and more brain cells are destroyed or compromised, the brain loses the ability to direct life-giving functions in the body, and the patient dies.

More than five million Americans are estimated to have Alzheimer's or similar forms of dementia, of which there are over fifty types, although as many as half may not be formally diagnosed. Often, those afflicted are able to cope well enough to cover up the early signs, or a spouse becomes adept at compensating for them. Fortunately, Medicare's new annual wellness visit pays for cognitive screening: simple, noninvasive tests that signal who should be referred for more extensive exams. Again, your health care provider is your best source of information.

The spectrum from natural signs of aging, to mild cognitive impairment, to advanced dementia or Alzheimer's is a broad one. Only careful observation and assessment can help you know exactly where your parent falls on this spectrum. Early diagnosis is important, because while current treatments won't stop Alzheimer's from progressing, they can slow the process of deterioration significantly.

As Baby Boomers begin to sense changes in brain function, it's not unusual to hear a comment like, "I'm so sorry I forgot our lunch date. I think I may be getting Alzheimer's." Those with loved ones who have Alzheimer's can tell you it is heartbreaking and nothing to joke about.

Walking into a beloved parent's room and realizing they have no idea who you are can be devastating. Michelle S. Bourgeois, a speech pathology professor at Ohio State University, developed a tool to help. "Your mother will never forget you," Bourgeois suggested to one heartbroken daughter named Susan. "She just needs help remembering." The solution was for Susan to give her mom two photos: one labeled, "This is my daughter Susan at age three," and the other labeled, "This is my daughter Susan now." The aging mother studied the two photos, then looked at her daughter and said, "As beautiful as ever." The visual and written cues were the keys because, according to Bourgeois, spoken words tend to literally go in one ear and out the other. This is why Alzheimer's patients tend to ask the same question again and again.[7]

While caring for someone you love who has Alzheimer's disease can be challenging and heartbreaking, it can also bring surprising gifts. A friend at church confided in me that she never really had a very close relationship with her demanding mother. But once her mother slipped into the fog of Alzheimer's, her critical attitude toward her daughter disappeared, and what was left was the tenderness and love that had really been there beneath the criticism all along.

Sue, another friend, said that her father was pretty far along on his journey with Alzheimer's the night he gave her a special gift. Just before she left after visiting him at his facility, he stood up, put his hands on her shoulders, looked her in the eyes, and said, "I . . . love . . . you." He had been silent more and more, she said, making his effort to express his love all the more meaningful. "Needless to say, I burst into tears," Sue remembers. "We were able to communicate that night almost like old times, complete with his patting my shoulder and saying, 'There, there.'"

Humor is also an unexpected gift for some caring for Alzheimer's patients. "I entered my father's unit to hear the bellowing of a patient shouting, 'Where are my glasses?'" says Jane. The staff was searching for them. "My father came out of his room, smiling to see me, and I noticed he had on two pairs of glasses, one over the other." He was wearing his and his unit mate's. Never miss an opportunity like this one to laugh together over the situation. It makes crying together, when necessary, far more bearable.

New tests for predicting Alzheimer's are in the news often, but experts warn that none are conclusive, and they disagree on the value of such testing. While take-charge Baby Boomers may insist on being tested, most experts suggest that until there is a cure, we would be better off not labeling ourselves with this crippling disease prematurely. As it is, the Alzheimer's Association warns that unless a cure is developed, the Baby Boomer generation will be known as Generation Alzheimer's. Of all the ways we've been described, that isn't the description we would choose.

Also, diagnoses are not always accurate. Other medical conditions can present similar symptoms. People with brain tumors or normal pressure hydrocephalus (NPH), a condition that occurs when the clear fluid surrounding the brain fails to be reabsorbed, are in danger of not getting the treatment they need if an Alzheimer's diagnosis comes too quickly. Another danger of misdiagnosis is that it can result in depression, an even more common malady of aging.

Depression

Be aware of the difference between situational, temporary depression and a more serious, chronic depression. Temporary depression is commonly brought on by the loss of a spouse, a beloved pet, or even a drastic change like moving out of a lifelong home into a care facility.

"Depression is cumulative, and even small daily losses and changes can produce pervasive sadness that leads to depression," says counselor Dr. Helen B. McIntosh. Such depression can also be the result of undiagnosed illness. New activities, social interaction, and laughter can possibly have a positive impact on the temporarily depressed, whereas any attempts to cheer up the more seriously depressed may be fruitless.

The DSM-5, the diagnostic bible of the American Psychiatric Association, lists nine symptoms of depression and suggests that if five or more are present during the same two-week period then the patient may have a major depressive disorder.[8] Symptoms may include a change in personality, a depressed mood most of each day, and loss of interest or pleasure in previously enjoyed activities. Serious depression can interfere with healthy eating habits and sleep patterns, and eventually can render the elder incapable of functioning normally in daily life. Fortunately even chronic depression in elders can often be controlled or reversed with the proper medication, so watch carefully for signs of mood changes and encourage early intervention.

A sobering reason for not leaving depression untreated is that older adults have the highest suicide rate of any age group. There is one older adult suicide every ninety-five minutes in the United States, with older white men at greatest risk. It's speculated that because these men have the most status in our society, they have the most to lose as they age. Generationally speaking, they may also be less likely to talk about their feelings or seek help for depression.

In dealing with serious depression, adult children have to be bold and ask the hard questions: "Please tell me what's been going on with you." "Are you having any thoughts of hurting yourself? How would you do it?"[9] When it comes to suicide concerns, it's so much better to risk offending your parent than to do nothing and have him or her bring what may have been a wonderful life to a premature, tragic end. Double suicides of older couples also happen far too frequently, with double the heartache. If you even suspect suicidal tendencies in elders you love, seek help from suicide prevention centers or professionals in your community immediately.

Assessments

As in all areas of health care, accurate assessment is the key to accurate diagnosis in health care for the aging. A complete physical exam and blood work should be adequate for assessing physical health, but it may be more difficult to get an accurate cognitive assessment. Medical professionals can refer you to a neurologist or aging center where such assessments are routinely given. These noninvasive screenings can usually uncover and assess difficulties with memory, attention, and thinking as well as depression and anxiety.

If further testing is recommended, neuropsychological evaluations can delve deeper and uncover what may be causing a memory problem. They also assess the degree that medical problems such as stroke or head injury may be affecting cognitive abilities, as well as an individual's ability to complete important legal activities, manage finances, and perform other instrumental activities of daily living.

Sometimes families may resist testing because they don't want to face the results. And the results can be heartbreaking. My friend Sharon, who did want her mom tested, told me her saddest memory about her mom was "when she couldn't draw the face on a clock. This was a test to determine if her working memory was intact. I just cried and cried."

Cost is a consideration in getting some of these assessments, I know, but sending someone you love down the wrong path of care or treatment is far more costly. Remember too that conditions in the mind and body can change rapidly in elders. Ask care providers which assessments should be administered annually, and keep accurate records of what needs to be done when. Many of these assessments are billed on a sliding income scale or covered by Medicare and other health care plans, but check first. Regardless, it is money well spent.

Having sharp minds as long as we live is the goal for most of us, and certainly it's our desire for the parents we love. But it's important to remember that people are not diminished because of afflictions of the brain. Under the cloud of confusion, they are still the same people they always were. We may just have to work a bit harder to see them and communicate with them. A beautiful quote by Henry Wadsworth Longfellow seems to cast the right light on this situation: "For age is opportunity no less than youth itself, yet in another dress. And as the evening twilight fades away, the sky is filled with stars, invisible by day." Don't miss the stars.

Chapter 8

LIVING WITH THE AGING BODY

Therefore we do not lose heart. Though outwardly we are wasting away, yet inwardly we are being renewed day by day.
—2 Corinthians 4:16

We received a call that my mother-in-law, usually so lucid, was acting strangely and seemed confused about both who she was and where she was. We already suspected that she suffered from sundowners, the condition common in some elders to be less oriented later in the day, but the symptoms she was manifesting now were more extreme.

After a bit of discussion and investigation, my brother-in-law asked that she be tested for a urinary tract infection. It turned out that was the cause, and after a day on medication she was back to normal. Who knew that a urinary tract infection could cause confusion? Certainly geriatricians know, but not inexperienced caregivers like us. For me, it was one more sign of the strong connection between mind and body—especially as we age.

You've heard the expression about old age being a question of mind over matter: if you don't mind, it doesn't matter. Some seniors adopt that attitude toward their aging bodies and are able to go right ahead and do whatever they want, regardless of any ailments or physical limitations.

"In God's eyes, the sunset is just as beautiful as the sunrise," read a sign in an assisted living facility I toured. It brought tears to my eyes. Our elders may be in the sunset of their lives, but they are still children of God, created in His image and imbued with a unique blend of characteristics, skills, and attributes that will be with them until their dying breath. It's our job to remind them of who they are on those days when the image they see in the mirror is of some old person they don't recognize.

But we can't help or encourage effectively unless we empathize. At a fund-raising banquet for Crossroads Ministries USA, a ministry to the elderly based in Colorado Springs, guests were asked to put cotton balls in their ears and gauzy masks over their eyes to simulate aging. How relieved we were when we could remove both after only a few minutes, but the exercise succeeded in increasing our empathy.

Researchers at the Massachusetts Institute of Technology's AgeLab developed a program called AGNES, which stands for Age Gain Now Empathy System. It revolves around an old person suit that simulates what it feels like to be seventy-five years old with arthritis and diabetes.

"The business of old age demands new tools," said Joseph Coughlin, AgeLab director. "While focus groups, observations and surveys can help you understand what the older consumer needs and wants, young marketers never get that 'Aha!' moment of having difficulty opening a jar, or getting in and out of a car. That's what AGNES provides."

From head to toe, those wearing the suit experience three things many seniors experience daily: fatigue, friction, and frustration. Special shoes provide a feeling of imbalance, while braces on the knees and elbows limit joint mobility. Gloves give the illusion of decreased strength and mobility in the hands and wrists, and earplugs make it difficult to hear. AGNES has been used by a group of students working on an updated walker as well as by clothing companies, car companies, and retail goods companies to help them understand the limitations of an older consumer.[1]

We may be the "just do it" generation, but that philosophy only goes so far as we reach out to help the elders we love. We need to empathize before we can encourage. We also need to be keenly aware of the connection between the mind and the body. Don't we all hope that our own minds and bodies will wear out at about the same time? We fear having a sharp mind in a body that's failing, or a strong body left without a functioning brain to control it. In caring for older adults, we may be faced with one of these scenarios. Several times I have witnessed the power of the mind-body connection in older adults struggling to hold on to this life in spite of their failing bodies. Once their minds accept that the battle is lost, however, death quite naturally follows.

So how long can we expect to live? How long will our seniors need our help before they get to leave their earthly tents and move into mansions in heaven? Only God knows. As I often tell the assisted living residents I share devotions with each week, "You may assume that because I am younger than you are that you will get to heaven ahead of me. But I could easily pull out in front of a truck when I leave here today and arrive there way before you." No one knows. It's better for each of us to live every day as fully and joyfully as we can—just in case it's our last.

Yet statistics and personal health histories give us general guidelines about life expectancy. The most recent information, according to data compiled by the Social Security Administration, is that a man reaching age sixty-five in the United States today can expect to live, on average, until age eighty-four. A woman turning sixty-five can expect to live until age eighty-six. Those are just averages, though.

About one out of every four sixty-five-year-olds today will live past age ninety, and one out of ten will live past age ninety-five.[2] The US Census Bureau reported that in 2010 we had 53,364 centenarians living in the United States. Given improvements in medical care and nutrition, that number will only grow.

All these averages are affected by factors such as race, gender, current health, lifestyle, and family history, all of which can increase or decrease life expectancy.

Perhaps more pertinent to the question of how long we will be caring for our elder parents is a perspective Gail Sheehy stated in her book *New Passages*. "The average American woman can expect to spend more years caring for her parents than she did caring for her children," she wrote.[3] That's sobering news for many of us.

It's foolish to make concrete plans about ourselves or others based on statistics and conjecture, however. We don't know how long we or our elderly parents will live. Rather than speculate, it's better to heed the words of Psalm 90:12: "Teach us to number our days, that we may gain a heart of wisdom." Reflecting on this verse, Charles R. Swindoll wrote, "When I can live it God's way, as prescribed here in Psalm 90:12, I take that day as His gift to me, which I live under His control and for His glory."[4]

We pray our elders will embrace Swindoll's philosophy, but what's our role in helping them to live every day to its fullest—and to God's glory? We all want to be wise when it comes to making decisions, or even suggestions, that impact the mental and physical health of elders we cherish. Yet we live in a society with a glut of information and, it sometimes seems, a dearth of really helpful direction.

It is impossible within these pages to provide all the information you need to make sound decisions. Obviously you will rely most heavily on physicians and caregivers you trust and on the research you do on any malady that presents itself. What I can do, however, is increase your awareness by outlining some general changes that tend to accompany aging, and by suggesting where you might look for help.

Health Care Options

Finding the right health care professionals is critical. Make the extra phone calls, ask the person behind you in line in the grocery store, do whatever you have to do to find health care providers who are familiar with the mind-body connection and with the special problems of the aging. A general practitioner your elder trusts who has many geriatric patients in his or her practice could be a good choice. Otherwise, search for geriatricians (medical doctors specializing in treating the elderly) who come highly recommended by other families. Other specialists who may be available in larger cities include geropsychologists and geroneurologists—both specializing in treating older adults.

Many elders, especially those with limited incomes, are fortunate to have PACE facilities in their communities. PACE stands for Program for All-Inclusive Care for the Elderly and is committed to helping participants achieve their highest level of independence by utilizing a coordinated team approach to health care, providing the entire continuum of care to seniors with chronic care needs. Most services are underwritten by grants from nonprofits or are nominal in cost, and transportation to and from the PACE location is often provided. Elders in the assisted living community where I volunteer get excited when it's their day to be picked up by the PACE bus, and they return full of conversation and laughter about their experience. You simply can't put a price on that kind of success.

Regardless of what health care you are able to find, never underestimate the importance of keeping careful records, accompanying elders to doctor appointments to take notes, asking the hard questions, following up on treatment plans, and, in short, simply being the patient advocate we all need when we ourselves are infirm. This may be a role you never applied for and never wanted, but if it falls on you, God will give you the grace to be the advocate your elder needs. Few roles you have in life will be as frustrating—or as fulfilling.

Medication

In considering the connection between the aging mind and the aging body, it's important to discuss the effects of medication on our elders, because medication affects both. Many elders are able to live healthy lives for much longer because of getting exactly the medicine they need, but for those caring for older adults, determining what is truly needed is a constant challenge.

On average, nine to thirteen prescriptions a month are filled by a senior adult. Drugs to control blood pressure, cholesterol, heart conditions, depression, digestion, pain, etc., can build up in the older adult because the kidneys aren't filtering as fast as they used to. Adverse drug reactions are the fifth largest cause of death in the elderly, and 30 percent of hospitalizations of the elderly are due to adverse drug reactions.

The "prescribing cascade" effect—that is, one medication leads to others to manage side effects—is frequent with older adults. This population is also seven times more likely to use over-the-counter medications than the average adult, and they often don't tell their doctors about these and other herbal supplements. They don't think these things matter since they aren't prescribed. But some supplements can interact with prescribed medicines. For instance, St. John's Wort interacts negatively with pain medications, and Benadryl, which some seniors take to get a good night's sleep, reverses the effect of dementia-reducing drugs.

We often hear about the hazards of going to several specialists, each prescribing different medications but not always checking to see what the patient is already taking. Until this is solved through some sort of universal record-keeping system within the medical profession, it's imperative for seniors and those who accompany them to the doctor to keep an accurate list of all medications the elderly are taking—prescribed, over-the-counter, and supplemental—along with the dosage of each, and present it to each physician. Overmedicating is a common problem in older adults. So often near the end of a person's life, once a terminal illness is diagnosed, medications are withdrawn and the family observes clarity of mind they haven't seen in their aging adult in years. It's a delicate balance.

Another tip for managing medications wisely is to select a pharmacist you trust who works with your elder's health care insurance. Go to this same source for all medications. Due to the shortage of family doctors, pharmacists are doing more and more consulting and may be the most likely to identify a potentially harmful drug interaction before it happens.[5]

If your mom or dad is still able to keep up with his or her own medications, don't underestimate the effectiveness of a well-labeled pill box (available at any drugstore or grocery store). Some have compartments for each day of the week, and some are broken down further by morning, midday, and evening. One of our chores when we visited my mother-in-law weekly was to go through her prescriptions and divide up what she was to take each day into two pill boxes—blue for daytime, orange for before bed. This helped her keep things straight for several years. Her home health care worker was not licensed to dispense medications, but when we noticed something was running low we could renew the prescription and she could pick it up later. Those simple plastic pill containers made our system possible.

Falls and Broken Bones

Most elderly adults do everything they can to avoid a fall. Exercise classes that include balance and coordination are a wonderful idea for fall prevention, and many senior centers offer them. Just holding on to a counter with one hand and standing on one foot, then the other, is a beginning exercise almost any elder may be able to accomplish.

So often a fall, and the broken bone or injury that can result, is a game-changer in the life of an older adult. You may be reading this book right now because your mom or dad fell, and the decision about whether this loved one could continue living alone was made the minute that dear elderly body hit the floor.

My mother-in-law's first significant fall was a doozy. She had a special group of friends her age who often went out to brunch together after church—the highlight of her social life most weeks. One day a member of the group invited everyone to her home for lunch. An elderly gentleman picked Mary Frances up to take her. As they were leaving the residence that day, she exited without waiting for someone to take her arm and missed a step on the front porch. Down she went onto the concrete sidewalk, catching herself with her hands.

Her wrists hurt when she got home, but she decided she was fine, took a couple of aspirin, and went to bed. In the morning she realized she couldn't push herself up to get out of bed. Somehow, however, she was able to pick up the phone on her bedside table and call a neighbor. My husband got the call that she was being taken to the ER and immediately drove the forty miles to intercept her there. The X-rays taken revealed two severely broken wrists, and Mary Frances went into surgery the same day.

I wish I could accurately describe the appliances used to piece her wrists back together. Imagine the parallel bars on which gymnasts perform. Now imagine these bars sticking out of each of your arms. Two vertical metal tubes connected by one horizontal tube were sticking up a few inches from each arm. Yet I have a lovely photo of Mary Frances flashing her million dollar smile as she sat in a chair in her hospital room the day after the surgery. She said it didn't really hurt to have metal bars attached to her bones and sticking out of her arms, but we were in pain just seeing the torturous-looking apparatuses.

Operating in crisis mode, my husband spent the better part of the next two days interviewing doctors and pastors to select the best rehabilitation facility available for his mom's recovery in her hometown. We moved her there, but to say we were less than pleased with "the best" is an understatement. The pain came later, and Mary Frances complained that when she rang for medication, it took over an hour for her to get it. One day we sat in a meeting where an administrator at this facility told us, "Elderly people get confused about time. It probably was only about five to ten minutes." Fortunately, at an earlier visit I had timed how long it took for someone to respond. Mary Frances was right. The administrator was wrong.

On another visit, I saw her lunch tray sitting next to her bed, completely untouched. "Weren't you hungry?" I asked. "Well, they brought it in and left it, but I can't cut anything up, so I couldn't eat it," she responded with resignation. Do you not think they could notice those bars sticking out of her arms and ask her if she needed help eating? Like us, you may find yourself in the position of feeling you must monitor every action, ask every obvious question, in order for your elderly patient to get the care he or she needs. I hope not, because it's a frustrating situation.

Mary Frances eventually healed to the point of getting the appliances removed. (My husband could tell you the details of that harrowing doctor appointment. It included the surgeon saying he needed to go out to his car to get a wrench.) She returned home, with in-home health care, and was able to stay there two more years before a fall down the steps sent her to assisted living. But it was a fall in her assisted living apartment, resulting in a broken hip, that precipitated the end of her marvelous life.

It's amazing how many well-meaning peers, when they hear your mom broke a hip, will say, "Oh, that's the beginning of the end." That may be, but it's not what you need to hear when you are in the midst of organizing her care and trying to keep her spirits up—and yours. Orthopedists explain that while it is certainly possible to fall and break a hip, it's likelier for the hip to simply give out and break, or slip out of its old socket, and then the elderly person falls. Regardless, the results are the same: a broken bone and more decisions to make.

Once again my husband and I were in crisis mode, trying to decide what course of action to take. Did it make sense to replace the hip of a ninety-one-year-old? The surgeon advised that even if Mary Frances were bedridden for the rest of her life, she would be more comfortable sitting up in bed with an intact hip joint, so she and we opted for a partial hip replacement. She came through the surgery well, went into skilled nursing, but passed away two weeks later—less than a week after her ninety-second birthday. The broken hip had in fact been the beginning of the end. But this will not be true for every senior whose hip breaks.

Most of us are aware that we lose bone density as we age—as much as 50 percent by age seventy, according to one estimate. Osteopenia, bone mass density that is lower than normal, can progress to mild, moderate, or severe osteoporosis—at which point fractures are more common for the simple reason that soft bones break more easily than hard bones. (Interestingly, arthritis causes a hardening of the bones, so people with arthritis rarely get osteoporosis.)

In recent years, Baby Boomers have been coached by practitioners and physiologists to care for their bones by doing weight-bearing exercises, taking calcium and Vitamin D, refraining from smoking, and eating healthily. Still, regularly scheduled bone density tests may show a continuous loss of bone mass even in patients who follow all the guidelines. Genetics plays a huge role, and some doctors advise female Boomers who want to predict their future bone health to look at their mothers.

How well any of us recover from a broken bone or joint replacement depends in part on two factors: our mental status and how fit we are overall. Maintaining a healthy lifestyle and encouraging the same in our elders is no wasted effort; however, neither is it a foolproof guarantee of strong bones.

Exercise

Any exercise is better than no exercise at all for older adults. Exercise improves the appetite, aids in digestion, stimulates the brain, keeps stiff joints working, and increases balance to prevent falls. My mother never exercised on purpose, but her room in assisted living was as far from the dining room as it could be, so several times a day she took a nice, long walk there and back.

I once heard an interviewer ask the actress Betty White how she stayed so fit into her late eighties. She said she lived in a three-story house, and she was very forgetful! Any walking helps, and climbing stairs safely is great exercise.

Unfortunately, for every octogenarian who still plays golf, lifts weights, or skis, there are many more who have given up on movement and let their muscles atrophy. First they find it difficult to stand up from a chair unassisted; the walker and wheelchair often follow. Exercise doesn't guarantee our seniors won't spend years in a wheelchair at the end of life, but it sure increases the odds in their favor. Encourage the older adults you love to walk around the grounds where they live, to stretch daily, and to participate in whatever exercise classes are offered. Use it or lose it applies to our bodies as well as our minds.

Nutrition

Fortunately for our society, the importance of good nutrition has never been more loudly proclaimed. Our food choices are sometimes overwhelming as food producers try to cater to wheat-free, gluten-free, low-fat, low-sodium, and vegetarian or vegan diets.

Yet many older adults still suffer from poor nutrition for a variety of reasons. Those who live alone may find it difficult to prepare nutritious meals due to limited vision or mobility, and a general lack of motivation may ensue. Older adults don't require as many calories as younger adults, so every calorie they consume must be packed with the right nutrients in order for diet alone to sustain them.

Often an elder who lives alone may seem lethargic and depressed, all because of poor eating habits. We finally convinced my mother-in-law to sign up for a meal delivery service for seniors in her community. Within two weeks, we noticed a significant improvement in her well-being. Her meal arrived at noon each day, at which time she ate most of it, saving the soup and dessert for her evening meal. Not only did she enjoy the variety, but she also perked up when her favorite delivery volunteer, a caring and friendly man, came to the door. He brought her more than food—he brought cheer and friendship. Most communities have nonprofit or government-run meal programs for seniors. It's a call worth making.

"As we get older, the body becomes less efficient at absorbing some key nutrients," says Katherine Tucker, RD, PhD, chair of the department of health sciences at Northeastern University in Boston. Our ability to taste food also declines, blunting appetite. Some foods become difficult to chew or digest. Key nutrients which may be in short supply in an older person's diet include vitamin B12, folic acid, calcium, vitamin D, potassium, magnesium, and fiber. A well-rounded diet high in fruits and vegetables can meet many of these needs. Some seniors enjoy getting many of these nutrients from easy-to-drink smoothies.

A diet that includes adequate fiber—found in whole grains, nuts, beans, fruits, and vegetables—removes the need for laxatives and/or stool softeners, which are often prescribed to counteract the effects of medications.

Water is also important for keeping older bodily systems working well, and many seniors suffer from illnesses brought on by nothing more than dehydration. The sense of thirst may decline as we age, so adult children and caregivers should remind seniors to drink at least three to five glasses of water a day. A suggestion: if the senior has a refrigerator, stock it with small, four-ounce water bottles, which seem more inviting and less challenging to finish than larger bottles. Loosen the caps if necessary. Of course some seniors may have conditions that restrict their fluid intake, or they may be taking prescribed diuretics. As with all aspects of care, work with your health care provider to achieve the best nutrition plan for the elder you love—and get ready to do some gentle coaching.[6]

Documents

Legal documents that should be in place as your senior ages can be a touchy topic. Nevertheless, as with driving, you must take a deep breath and gently approach the discussion about advance medical directives to be used in the event your loved one can no longer make his or her wishes known due to dementia, coma, or other conditions. These legal documents vary slightly from state to state. An online search will tell you what your state requires and may even provide the forms you need to fill out and have notarized. Patient representatives in doctor's offices, care centers, and hospitals can often help as well. There are three primary types of documents to consider. (Incidentally, anyone can be in an end-of-life situation, not just the elderly, so these documents are recommended for all of us.)

- Living Will (also known as Health Directive): This document spells out what life-sustaining measures and treatments you do and do not want, including the use of ventilators (life support) or feeding tubes.
- Medical or Healthcare Power of Attorney: This document designates a trusted person to act as the senior's representative or proxy to make health care decisions for the patient in the event that he or she is unable to do so. This can be a family member but in some situations it's wiser to choose a trusted younger friend. It should probably be someone living in close proximity. One note here if you are the one overseeing hospitalization: Medicare pays for rehabilitation only for people admitted to a hospital for three or more days as inpatients. It does not pay if the patient's status is listed as "under observation." Inquire and make sure your patient's status is listed correctly. It could save thousands of dollars in extra medical costs.
- Do Not Resuscitate (DNR): This document states that the patient does not wish to have cardiopulmonary resuscitation (CPR) if his or her heart stops or he or she stops breathing. Very elder seniors are highly advised to have this directive in place, because CPR can not only bring them back to a life of

suffering but also result in painful broken ribs. In some states, the patient need not create a separate DNR document but can simply request that a doctor enter the preference into the medical chart.

If the senior you know has a pacemaker, remember to discuss end-of-life preferences with your health care provider about removal or deactivation. There are gruesome stories of older adults who were ready to die but were prevented from doing so by their pacemakers, which painfully jolted them again and again. My friend Kathy's father, Ed, had a defibrillator/pacemaker combination installed. It served him well for years, but when he was in failing health, it once fired off twenty times in thirty minutes. Each time felt like an electrocution or "like being kicked by a horse." As Kathy said, "When the Lord is trying to call you home, it keeps you alive." During his last visit to the ER, he asked that the device be turned off, and the ER doctor complied. Ed lived another two months.

It's wise to make sure that primary physicians, frequented hospitals, and care centers keep copies on file of these formalized documents and any other directives written into medical records. The patient and the primary caregiver should also have copies. Too often, the right provider doesn't have access to the right document at the right time, so duplication helps.

An organization called Aging with Dignity created an all-in-one advance directive document titled "Five Wishes" that is recognized in most states. In this single document, which must be notarized, the senior specifies the following:

- The person I want to make decisions for me when I can't
- The kind of medical treatment I want or don't want
- How comfortable I want to be
- How I want people to treat me
- What I want my loved ones to know

This is a great tool for Baby Boomers to fill out now, so have a Five Wishes party with your seniors and do it all together. Call 888-5-WISHES for the forms.

Another helpful form is called MOST: Medical Orders for Scope of Treatment. It summarizes a patient's wishes and travels with the patient between facilities—a very useful concept. Ask if it is used in your state.

Many seniors do not carry life insurance policies into old age, as the purpose of such a policy is to replace lost income to provide for a spouse or family. After retirement, needs change or are met in other ways. However, a discussion and a decision about long-term health insurance are still necessary.

Offsetting the high costs of long-term care appeals to many families. However, this industry is rapidly changing, and the only way to know if it's the right choice for your aging parent—or for yourself—is to visit with an insurance broker you trust and weigh the financial pros and cons. Plans differ widely in coverage, and some companies seem unreasonably reluctant to pay benefits.

My sisters kept trying to get my mom qualified for benefits on a plan she had been paying on since she was fifty-nine. Unfortunately, every time someone from the insurance company came to interview her, Mom would put on her perkiest smile and say, "No, I'm fine! I don't need any help at all!" In order to qualify, the insured must need help with daily activities like dressing, toileting, bathing, transferring from a chair to a bed, mobility, and medication management. My mom did need help with some of these things but didn't want to admit it. Consequently, she didn't receive benefits from her long-term care policy until six months before she died.

Such tenacity isn't all bad, though. It empowers elders to live long and healthy lives. My mom never formally exercised a day in her life. Her diet consisted primarily of Southern fried foods. She sipped a bourbon and water almost every night and was in amazingly good health until near the end of her life. She was almost ninety-three when she died. Was it good genes or sheer determination? I don't know. I only know her lifestyle worked for her.

"In spite of illness, in spite even of the archenemy sorrow, one can remain alive long past the usual date of disintegration if one is unafraid of change, insatiable in intellectual curiosity, interested in big things, and happy in small ways," Edith Wharton wrote in *A Backward Glance*.[7] A healthy mind and body are key components of healthy aging, no doubt, but again and again we see elders who demonstrate that what matters most is attitude. They know that what brings joy to life is the indefatigable spirit within.

Chapter 9

STAYING YOUNG AT HEART

*They will still bear fruit in old age,
they will stay fresh and green.*
—Psalm 92:14

America seems to have an ongoing love affair with the oldsters among us who live out their lives with a lot of passion—and huge amounts of heart. Hardly a month goes by when there isn't an article in our local paper about a centenarian celebrating a birthday in one of our care centers. Recently there was a story about a gentleman, 106, shown at his party giving a two-year-old a seat on his walker.

The photo in another article shows Elsa Bailey snow skiing at Arapahoe Basin—the only Colorado ski area that still had snow in May—on her one hundredth birthday. She had been a skier for seventy years, starting on the icy slopes of Massachusetts on a pair of seven-dollar skis, and taking a few more turns down the hill before hanging up her skis for good was her idea of celebrating in style.

"Life is good. Life is interesting," Elsa told the reporter. "All you have to do is enjoy it. I was told long ago that it's not what happens that makes you happy, it's what you decide. You can be sick and if you want to be happy, all you have to do is turn on the happy machine and everything's fine. So I try to turn on the happy machine as often as I can. I've had a very good and interesting life. I'm very fortunate."

The article goes on to say that Elsa's future plans include seeing the fjords in Norway, the polar bears in the Arctic, and Yellowstone National Park.[1] Elsa may have given up skiing, but not adventure.

Of course, now we can not only read about elders doing amazing things, but we can also see them accomplishing their feats on YouTube. One of my favorite video clips is titled "Mathilda's Solo." In it, Mathilda, ninety-four, comes out onto the dance floor with a walker. She's dressed in a trench coat and has a plastic rain hat on her head (the same kind my mom always kept folded up in her purse). The music begins, Mathilda's dance partner removes Mathilda's hat and coat to reveal her flapper outfit, and the two of them begin ballroom dancing with moves that could get them into the finals of *Dancing with the Stars*. Watch it anytime you need to give yourself a boost.

And you mustn't miss seeing the YouTube clip of the Sun City Poms strutting their stuff. This senior cheerleading squad has been performing since 1979, and the only requirement is that members be over fifty-five years old. Many are in their seventies and two are octogenarians. They engage their minds by learning new routines and their bodies by practicing three times a week. They perform up to fifty shows a year, including parades and pep rallies.

"Being in the Poms, I think you really have to push yourself," said Nancy Walker, sixty-four, in an interview. "You have to get out of your comfort zone and do something you didn't think you could ever do." My favorite quote came from Pat Weber, eighty-two. She didn't join the Poms when she first wanted to because her husband forbade it, and she respected his wishes.

"He said, 'over my dead body,' so I thought well, all right I don't want to rock the boat, I just won't do it. And then, shortly after that, he passed away . . . so I came and joined the Poms."[2]

It may be fun and inspiring for you and the elders you love to look at videos or newspaper reports of older people who smash the stereotypes of aging. But there is a delicate balance. We want to encourage our seniors to be all that they can be, but we *don't* want them to feel inadequate because they can't ski, dance, or cheer. They don't want to be compared to their peers any more than we wanted to be asked, "Why can't you be more like your brother?" when we were growing up.

Our goal is to remind our aging parents of the things that make them uniquely themselves and to do all we can to help them keep their personhood intact. One of my favorite photos of my mom after she moved into assisted living was taken by the activities director the day Mom was elected Valentine Queen. Mom didn't have to dance the quickstep to be elected or enter a bathing suit competition. The residents voted for her because of who she always was: an outgoing, gregarious woman with a great sense of humor who genuinely enjoyed interacting with others and making their day better. In the photo, she's wearing a bejeweled tiara, holding a red scepter, and sporting a hot pink feather boa around her neck. There is a dazzling smile on her face. That day, and always, she had a whole lot of heart.

You Gotta Have Heart

So what does it mean to have heart? A poignant example is found in the small but powerful book *Two Old Women* by Velma Wallis. Based on an Athabascan Indian legend passed along for many generations from mothers to daughters of the upper Yukon River Valley in Alaska, it's the inspirational tale of two old women abandoned by their tribe during a brutal winter famine. The chief regrets having to leave the old women behind, as do the families of the elders, but the decision is made that they must be abandoned so the others can move on.

What happens next should encourage all of us who aren't as young and capable as we once were. "We have learned much during our long lives," said one of the women named Sa'. "Yet there we were in our old age, thinking that we had done our share in life. So we stopped, just like that. No more working like we used to, even though our bodies are still healthy enough to do a little more than we expect of ourselves."[3]

Her slightly older friend, Ch'idzigyaak, listened carefully to her friend's revelation as to why they were left behind.

"Two old women," Sa' continued. "They complain, never satisfied. We talk of no food, and of how good it was in our days when it really was no better. We think that we are too old. Now, because we have spent so many years convincing the younger people that we are hopeless, they believe that we are no longer of use to this world." And then she lays down a challenge for herself and her friend: "If we are going to die anyway, let us die trying!"[4]

By the end of the book, the two old friends have done more than try—they have survived, and survived beautifully. So successful are they in employing all the wisdom and skills they accumulated over their many decades that when they are eventually reunited with the tribe, they have pelts and food to share with those who walked off and left them to die.

The lesson is one we can apply to helping our aging parents. Without unmercifully nagging them into doing everything they once could do, we need to gently encourage them to do what they still can. How often we hear of people dying shortly after retirement simply because they feel their life is over. Likewise, older adults can simply give up once they are moved into an assisted living facility if those around them treat them as though they can't do anything for themselves anymore. Better to err on the side of encouragement than discouragement. And when necessary, simply take their hands again.

In her book titled *10 Gospel Promises for Later Life*, author Jane Marie Thibault references a study conducted by Robert C. Peck that outlined three developmental tasks of later life: (1) learning to appreciate oneself as a unique person rather than as a worker; (2) learning to transcend and live with inevitable aches and pains and other physical diminishment rather than becoming preoccupied with one's body; and (3) learning to go beyond one's own small ego needs to respond to the needs of the larger community and the next generation. Those are goals you can gently encourage your elders to adopt just as you encourage them to accept their losses graciously and live in the moment.[5]

All of these tasks fall into the "easier said than done" category for many seniors, but they also describe a life lived to its fullest, a life lived with heart. Like the old women in the story, older people who practice them never give up on living until the Lord calls them home. It's not that they don't have aging brains and bodies; they just choose not to be defined by their frailties. Our generation had better get this right, because some of us could have twenty-five or thirty years left to live after retirement. We need to finish well. "Aging isn't a choice. But our response to it is," said Charles R. Swindoll. "In so many ways we ourselves determine how we shall grow old."[6]

So what sorts of activities and opportunities help our elders hold on to who they are and live a life with heart? The best of the senior centers and facilities offer many options. Exercise classes, shopping excursions, and book or discussion groups may be the most prevalent, but golf, pickle ball, tennis, and dance classes are not out of the question. Willing residents and participants make the most of what's offered. To live a life with heart is to choose joy and share it with others. It's to find beauty and purpose in what others see as old and worn. And so we say *"L'chaim!"*—"To life!"

Growing old with heart means choosing to *live* for as long as we are alive. It means being present in the moment and looking for those activities, people, or animals that bring out who we really are. It's holding on to a youthful attitude while engaging in life in as many ways as possible.

My friend Pat and her husband drove to the next state to take

Pat's Aunt Marthelle out to eat on her one hundred first birthday. The wait staff sang to her and told all the other diners her age. Later a gentleman came over to the table to congratulate Aunt Marthelle. "My mother is with us," he said, "and she's one hundred and six." When he walked away, Aunt Marthelle muttered under her breath, "Yeah, well, she looks it too." Marthelle has spunk, humor, *and* heart!

In the heartwarming movie *Quartet* about retired opera singers living together in a lovely British retirement home with lush gardens, an exchange between two of the residents reveals the difference attitude can make. When her longtime friend asks the character Jean Horton, played by Maggie Smith, to sing with the others in an upcoming gala, Jean refuses. Explaining that she has lost her gift, she says, "You must understand. I was someone once." Without missing a beat, her friend Cissy, played by Pauline Collins, retorts, "I thought I was someone now."[7] May our elders identify with Cissy, not Jean.

Casey Stengel said, "The trick is to grow old without getting old." Living with heart makes that possible.

Work and Volunteerism

As I go through the assisted living community rounding up residents for the weekly Bible study, I often find May in the dining hall. Lunch won't be served for another two hours, but there she sits in her wheelchair, using her feet to paddle from table to table. In her lap is a large basket of sugar packets, and it's her job to fill up the containers on each table, keeping the white packets separated from the pink artificial sweetener packets. She takes her job seriously. It gives her purpose.

May is extremely intelligent. Her earlier life was full of far more significant responsibilities. Neck pain almost paralyzes her some days and keeps her head curved downward. Yet she does what she can still do. She lives her life with heart.

In 1992, the television show *20/20* aired a segment titled "100 and Still Growing." The program's anchors were Hugh Downs and Barbara Walters, and I was so fascinated by their report that I ordered a transcript of the show. In the report, Downs introduced a study done of centenarians in Georgia by two professors, Leonard Poon and Gloria Clayton.

The researchers were asked if all the active hundred-year-olds they interviewed had anything in common. "We've uncovered four themes that exist among our entire sample," Clayton said, "and they are optimism, engagement or commitment to something they're interested in, activity or mobility, and the ability to adapt to loss."[8]

The first three of those four themes can be satisfied by finding a productive way to spend one's time either in the workforce or as a volunteer. Downs and Walters must have taken what they learned in this report seriously. Downs, ninety-three as of this writing, is still writing books and speaking, and Walters, eighty-five, retired from ABC's *The View* in 2014, but will no doubt contribute to network reports for many more years.

They are by no means the only aging seniors still working. A Gallup poll revealed that in 2013, 25 percent of Americans in the workforce were sixty-five and over. This is a 3 percent increase since 2010, perhaps due to a tight economy motivating more retirement-age people to keep their full-time jobs.[9]

A Massachusetts McDonald's honored one of its loyal employees for his twenty-five years of service on his one hundredth birthday! He hasn't been doing any heavy lifting since he hit his nineties. Rather, the manager pays him to chitchat with customers. The man, Morris Miller, received a certificate naming him "Crew Person of the Year" on his special day. The manager described him as "an ambassador for the brand," and Miller said, "I'll keep coming as long as I can move."[10]

Rose Syracuse, ninety-two, would still be working at Macy's in New York had she not broken her hip. She retired recently after working seventy-three years, mainly in the accounting department.

Technology didn't get the best of her; she learned "how to do the computer" in her seventies. The time just flew by, she says. "It didn't seem that long at all because you're happy at your job."[11]

Some seniors add late-in-life avocations to whatever they do as gainful employment. Longtime eldercare attorney Clifton Kruse Jr. began writing heartwarming stories based on the lives of his clients. He published his collection of writings in a book titled *Selma's Cat and Other Things That Matter* when he was in his seventies and still practicing law.

Retirees may return to fill valuable consulting positions and pass along the wisdom and knowledge only a life lived in the pursuit of knowledge can provide. Or they may find volunteering in their areas of expertise to be equally rewarding. Verne was a military band director for many years. Now he finds, repairs, and donates band instruments to middle schools and high schools—115 instruments to date. "Verne finds the whole endeavor to be very interesting and personally rewarding," his wife, Virginia, told me, "and the schools he assists are grateful for his contributions."[12]

Likewise retired schoolteachers volunteer in literacy programs and libraries, former executives provide business advice to entrepreneurs, and former bankers teach classes on managing personal finances. All bring enrichment to others and purpose to their own lives.

Learning and Technology

One thing that is guaranteed to keep us young at heart is to have a lifelong interest in learning something new—a curiosity that must be satisfied. I was once asked to mentor two young girls, fifth graders Laura and Aly, in creative writing. After the end of our semester together, I decided to show them the value of learning a craft that would last throughout their lives. I took them to meet my friend Denise, a former Chicago newspaperwoman, who in her eighties was still living in her home and still publishing stories and articles.

"My first memory of being a writer goes back to the three-story house I lived in with my family," Denise told the girls. "I would write a note to my sister who was down in the basement, and our dog Rags would take it down to her. Then she would write me a note back." (Then it was Rags, now it's email, but the process is the same.)

The girls had lots of questions for Denise. I was amazed at how much the four of us had in common in spite of our different generations, because we were all writers.

"Characterization comes easily to me," Denise told the girls, "but I really have trouble with plotting. I think I'm going to take a writing seminar on plotting to see if I can learn how to do it better."

I noticed the girls' eyes growing wider when Denise said she still wanted to learn something new. The lesson for all of us was that learning is a lifelong endeavor. It doesn't stop when school is out.

Author Jane Gross gives a poignant account of her elderly mom's desire to learn to write. Her mother hadn't been interested in any of the activities offered in the facility she reluctantly called home until they announced a seven-week class in creative writing.

"My mother's enthusiasm was instant and unmistakable," Gross says. "Here was an activity she actually wanted to do, the first since bridge had become more painful than pleasurable because of her crippled hands. She's always insisted she wasn't interested in the 'family business' of writing, but the gleam in her eye and the constant inquiries about when the class would start told me otherwise."[13]

A series of strokes made it seem unlikely that Gross's mother would be able to participate once the class started, but Gross describes her advocacy for her mother as akin to the Make-a-Wish Foundation advocating for a cancer victim. Ultimately a college intern was assigned to attend the class with Gross's mother, take notes, work on assignments, and translate for her when others couldn't understand what she was saying. It was a wonderful, fulfilling experience for them both.

All disciplines may be mastered by the masters of old age. The senior center in our community offers well-attended classes in all types of painting and drawing, nutrition, literature, bridge, and more. Every imaginable form of exercise is offered too, including yoga, tai chi, and Pilates. Dance classes include Zumba, aerobic dance, tap, and salsa.

Assisted living facilities can't always offer such a wide range of activities, but it's worth investigating what is offered so you can help your elder tap into something of interest. Like Jane Gross, you may have to do a bit of advocating, but most activities directors are interested in offering what residents want. See if there's a demand for whatever it is your elder wants to do, and make a request.

Technology is the new frontier into which many seniors with a thirst for learning venture. Connected Living is a cloud-based service that aims to make seniors more computer-savvy and allows them to bond with one another and their families through the Web. The Brookdale Senior Living Corporation has adopted this program for all their sites. Residents get email addresses, user-friendly Web browsing, Skype, and personal profiles highlighting their interests.

The reason for introducing technology to residents in assisted living is to help them make connections. Residents who feel less isolated will also feel less depressed and will engage more in other activities. So it's worth the hardware expense and the time for facilities to introduce technology to their residents now, before we Baby Boomers arrive with our smart phones and tablets and demand high-speed Internet. If a grandpa can see a new great-grandson in a state far away via Skype, or if two elderly sisters can stay in touch daily via email, then technology has a purpose for the aging.

Pursuit of Beauty

Proverbs 31:30 declares that "charm is deceptive, and beauty is fleeting; but a woman who fears the LORD is to be praised." The mature older women I've been blessed to know don't overvalue beauty or make it more important than their spiritual lives. But they still take pride in their appearance.

There were two things my mother wouldn't miss no matter what else was happening: her weekly bridge game and her hair appointment. And you'd have had more luck getting her to cancel bridge than hair. For most of her life, Mom wore her hair in a pouf-y French twist, and only Judy, her hairdresser across town, could style it to her liking. So my sisters dutifully took Mom to her appointments after she stopped driving. Why? Because it mattered to her. Like most care centers, Mom's had its own beauty parlor, but she wanted Judy and that was that.

At the assisted living facility where I volunteer, most of the ladies have standing appointments with the beautician who comes a few days a week, a young woman with many stars in her crown, I'm sure. I can always tell when someone has just had her hair done. Not only does she look pretty but her whole countenance is lifted.

Second in importance to hair are nails. Any woman can attest that a nice manicure and pedicure go a long way toward making you feel beautiful and more like yourself. Residents often compliment one another on their manicures—which are easily showcased at meals, card tables, and bingo games. Pedicures are more of a necessity than a luxury, however, as aging nails of both men and women can become extremely hard and difficult to clip. Encourage your elder to budget in regular hair and nail services. It's an investment neither of you will regret. A focus on outward appearance may seem superficial, but getting spiffed up is a morale boost at any age.

Music

Music is also a great mood elevator and a way to add joy—and heart—to the life of an elderly person. My sisters installed a Bose radio and CD player in my mother's apartment, and she had something playing all the time. Country music was her favorite, but classical music or jazz often transports oldsters back to when life seemed more melodic and serene, and it may put a bounce in their step.

If music has always been a part of your elder's life, do all you can to infuse as much of it as possible into each day. In an earlier chapter I mentioned Marion, who played the piano in her room so beautifully. When the former conductor of our local symphony moved into the assisted living community, he donated his personal piano to the dining room. Then Marion was able to play for the residents before and after meals, and they dearly loved it. Her memory for everyday tasks and relationships was failing her, but her musical memory was strong, and she played all the old hymns without sheet music.

Many seniors have rediscovered music through joining community glee clubs or bands. They may pick up a talent or instrument they had set aside earlier in life, or they may try something for the first time. Either way, music enriches their life.

Music is also therapy. An article in the *AARP Bulletin*, "The Power of Music," outlines all the ways music is used to communicate with Alzheimer's patients, stroke victims, and even those elders who have just shut down socially.

Geriatrician Theresa Allison, MD, told of an experience with her own grandmother. "I've watched her babble nonsense, but then bounce my son on her knee as we sing a folk song she taught me as a child. For 45 seconds life is completely normal," says Allison. "Engaging this way is profoundly meaningful." Therapists and caregivers are urged to select familiar songs—something the older person enjoyed in his or her twenties, for example. Some patients respond more favorably to directions that are sung rather than spoken, and just sitting and listening to music together can be a calming, bonding experience for elders and caregivers alike.[14]

A letter to the editor of the *Washington Post* poignantly demonstrates the power of music to tap into the memory:

> The patients in the Alzheimer's ward were seated in a circle, staring into space. I had come to engage them in their weekly sing-along, which I assumed had more effect on the health-care aides than on the patients. We sang old patriotic songs, which sometimes brought smiles to their faces. I ended with

their favorite, the rousing "Battle Hymn of the Republic." As I was packing to leave, an aide announced, "Everyone, please be quiet. Miss Betty would like to say something." A woman who had never said a word, stood up, straightened her shoulders and began: "I want to thank all my fellow graduates for coming here today. We have had four wonderful years together, but now must go out into the world." The music had prompted her to give her graduation address. I never again thought that I was leading singing sessions for people who didn't care. I couldn't tell from their behavior that these songs were affecting them, but now I knew that this music could take them back to happier times.[15]

On one of my visits to see my mom, a month before she passed away, we attended a live concert in her assisted living community. The music of the big band era filled the dining room, and Mom tapped her feet and swayed to the beat. She knew all the lyrics to all the songs. When they began to play "What a Wonderful World," the song made famous by Louis "Satchmo" Armstrong, Mom asked me to dance. Since men were in short supply, the women often danced together at these events, so we joined the group on the dance floor. I'm so glad the activities director captured a photo of us smiling and dancing to help me keep that moment alive in my heart and memory.

Mom never revealed to me that the dancing was hard on her physically, but on the way back to her room she casually said, "I'm going to stop in the nurse's office for a minute." I was able to peek through the door and saw the nurse giving Mom her "puffer" to help her breathing return to normal. Would it have been wiser for her to sit out that last dance we had together? Maybe. But then I wouldn't have the beautiful memory I have today, nor would I tear up every time I hear "What a Wonderful World." Her indomitable spirit and our last dance together were gifts my mom gave to me. She made it a wonderful world indeed.

Bingo, Bridge, and Such

The activities director at the assisted living center where I volunteer called to ask me if I would be willing to fill in for her and call a bingo game, and I was happy to do so. I had never called a bingo game before, but how hard could it be, right?

Wrong. It wasn't until the third game that one resident announced to the room that I wasn't doing it right. I was supposed to let several of the ping-pong balls fall out of the tumbler at once, *then* call out the numbers. I didn't know.

These regular Bingo players were serious about the game. They played for quarters, but cheating was not allowed—and not being able to hear the caller was no excuse for cheating.

Rather than sitting in their rooms watching game shows on television, the contestants were connecting with each other, showing me clearly the value in a competitive game of Bingo.

Card games are also popular with the senior set. My mom played bridge all of her adult life. On one of my visits after she'd moved to assisted living, it was her turn to hostess her bridge club. I helped her tidy her one-bedroom apartment where the group would gather first, and together we set up the luncheon table in the facility's activities room. Then Mom told me I was going to have to play bridge because one of the other ladies couldn't make it.

"Mother, I haven't played bridge in twenty-five years!" I protested.

"Oh, just sit there and hold the cards," she said. "It'll come back to you."

When Mom went down the list of who was coming, she arrived at one name that gave me a glimmer of hope. "Erma Jane has Alzheimer's," she said sadly, "but she can still play bridge, so we let her come. Her doctor says it's good for her."

Thinking I could at least play better than someone with Alzheimer's, I reluctantly agreed to fill in—and promptly found out I had a lot to learn besides the proper response to a short club bid. Erma Jane didn't remember the names of the lifelong friends she was playing with, and she tried to leave the activities room via a second-story balcony when the bridge game was over, but she bid and made a small slam, and she had no problem at all putting her opponents to shame, including me. The part of her brain that knew how to play bridge was still completely intact and functioning!

Some of these ladies I had known all my life. As a little girl, I had peeked into the living room to see their fashionable outfits and high heels when they came to our house for bridge club. Now that they were in their late eighties, everything took a little more time and a lot more effort, but they still looked their best, and they kept their minds engaged.

When I returned home I called up some friends of mine who also played bridge long ago, and we got together to see what we could remember. Amazed that it really did come back to us, we plan to follow the example of the "masters" of aging and keep playing for as long as we can.

Job 12:12 asks, "Is not wisdom found among the aged? Does not long life bring understanding?" When I consider the "master seniors" I know, I can only answer yes. It's not about playing bridge. It's about resting in the knowledge that, by the grace of God, you can make each day you live a day worth remembering. That's a lesson we amateurs need to take to heart.

Of course, bridge isn't the only card game seniors may remember and love. Two ladies in the assisted living community I frequent have a standing date, every day, to play gin rummy in the library. Don't even try to divert them to another activity. Neither can hear well enough to enjoy some of the other events, but boy do they love to play cards! (They don't need the playing cards with oversized numbers, but it's easy to find them if vision is a problem for your senior.)

Ann Hood wrote an essay for *Parade Magazine* simply titled "The Girls." In it she describes the regular Friday night poker games her mom and eleven friends faithfully attended for many, many years. They called themselves The Dirty Dozen until a few of them died;

then they just became The Girls. Eventually only the author's mom was left. Ann tried to engage her mom in learning to play bridge to fill the void but knew it wouldn't be the same. "How foolish I was to think that a new foursome could replace The Girls. I realized in that moment that there are some things for which there are no substitutes. There are some things that we must mourn and cherish and say good-bye to."[16] Yet the memories, and the laughter, remain.

If you're frustrated that the facility where your mom or dad lives doesn't seem to offer enough activities, consider volunteering your own talents to lead a book group, paint nails, facilitate a Bible study, or create craft projects. Most activities directors are overworked and would welcome the assistance. They may even be able to help with supplies. The blessings you receive will be well worth the effort. And besides, you're already there anyway, right? Add some heart.

Pet Therapy

A little dachshund lived with one of the residents where my mother-in-law resided. The dog's owner would shuffle along on her walker, and the little dog, old and grizzled of snout herself, would waddle along behind. Whenever we saw her or spoke to her, she would look up at us with the most soulful, pleading look in her eyes, as if to say, "Help me. Please. Why should I have to live here?"

Yet I'm sure this little dog was desperately loved and fulfilled a purpose in the life of her owner that she couldn't begin to understand. When pets are able to make the move with seniors into retirement homes or assisted living facilities, they bring so much comfort in the face of change.

Even visiting pets can add heart to the lives of residents. In her book *A Dog Walks into a Nursing Home*, Sue Halpern wrote about her experience taking her trained therapy dog, Pransky, to visit residents. Sue told *Parade Magazine*, "Innocence is lost when we stop seeing people for who they are and start seeing them for what they are—disabled, confused, frail. We allow ourselves to think of them as not simply older or less able, but 'other.'" Sue continues, "A dog does not understand 'other.' For Pransky, the attraction was elemental—it started with acceptance. It was her lesson and her gift to me, every single week."[17]

No wonder residents respond so warmly to visits from dogs, cats, and even llamas! Laura, ninety-five, has late-stage Alzheimer's, but she still loves to pet Travis the llama when he comes into the memory support unit at the Life Care Center of Nashoba Valley, in Littleton, Massachusetts. "She'll smile, she'll laugh," says her daughter Linda, "even if she doesn't recognize it's a llama."[18]

Wise caregivers know that pets can help elders tap into feelings and memories they wouldn't be able to access otherwise. A resident might see a dog that reminds her of a pet she had as a girl and begin an animated discussion about her life at that time. Holding and petting a dog or cat can also often soothe someone who's upset or disruptive in a memory care unit. The animal is a much more natural and healthier solution than a sedative.

You may remember accounts of Oscar, the tortoise-and-white cat living in a Rhode Island nursing home who kept vigil on the beds of patients who were about to die. Headlines reading "Cat Predicts Death" appeared in newspapers across the country in 2007. Over fifty cases of Oscar's accurate predictions were documented in a book written by geriatrician Dr. David Dosa titled *Making the Rounds with Oscar: The Extraordinary Gift of an Ordinary Cat*.

Naysayers argue that Oscar was only drawn to the room by the increased level of activity that surrounds a seriously ill person or because the body temperature of a dying person often elevates, making them a warm place to snuggle. But the nursing home staff feels differently and will inform the family of a patient if Oscar is lingering in the room—even if there are no other signs death is imminent. Families react with gratitude for Oscar's service. It comforts them to know Oscar was there with their loved one even if they couldn't get there in time themselves.

I don't know if Oscar has a special sense or just happens by at the right time, but I do know that if I'm near the end of my life, it would definitely comfort me to have my cats, Molly and Beau, curled up on the bed next to me. I would find their presence calming as I matched my labored breathing to the rhythm of their purring. Maybe Oscar has simply found his purpose in life.

Seniors still living on their own can have difficulty caring for pets, but please research options for help in your community before asking your elders to relinquish their best friends. Studies have documented a wide range of benefits for seniors who have animal companions, including a lessening of anxiety, lowering of blood pressure, and an emotional lift. Programs like the SPCA Senior Care Program in Sacramento, California, make it possible for even seniors with low income to keep their pets. Volunteers walk dogs, clean kitty litter boxes, administer medicine to pets, and even take them to the vet if necessary.[19]

Romance

Yes, hope and romance both spring eternal! Skilled nursing administrators and directors of assisted living communities are the first to report that gray hair isn't a sign of a lack of desire for love and romance. As the old joke states, just because there's snow on the roof doesn't mean the fire is out down below.

Your elder's love life may be the furthest thing from your mind, but you could be surprised. A friend of ours often dropped by to help her dad, an assisted living resident, with his personal finances. She was used to just popping into his room whenever she was in the area, so imagine her surprise the day she found him in a compromising position with one of the female residents.

"Dad, what are you doing?" she exclaimed.

"What does it look like I'm doing?" he replied. "Get out of my room."

As I mentioned before, my mom had a late-in-life fella, Cecil, who was special to her. But after they moved into assisted living residences in different states, they could only stay in touch by phone. When Cecil became ill, one of my sisters drove my mom from Tennessee to Georgia to see him. She said it broke her heart to see the two of them walking down the hall holding hands, knowing they wouldn't see one another again this side of heaven. Theirs was a platonic love but a true love nonetheless.

Unfortunately, some of the romantic encounters that occur in care facilities are not quite so sweet. Dementia can tap into basic desires, break down social mores, and cause a male or female resident to act inappropriately toward a member of the opposite sex. This is why you need to be alert to anything sexual that may be happening.

A retired nurse spoke frankly to my gerontology class about sexuality and aging. In her eighties, Marilyn Doenges put it this way: "We are sexual beings from birth to death. Our sexuality plays a significant role in our self-esteem, so there's no reason to abandon it in old age." She reminded us that it's possible to have intimacy without intercourse if the body stops functioning well sexually, because the brain is the most important sex organ.

According to Marilyn, 73 percent of seniors ages fifty-four through sixty-four engage in sexual relations, 50 percent of those ages sixty-five through seventy-five, and 26 percent of those ages seventy-five through eighty. Over ninety? She says some are "involved." She also shared a heart-stopping statistic. The fastest growing population for sexually transmitted diseases is over age sixty-five, primarily because older people didn't have to worry about such things when they were younger and first dating, and they certainly aren't worried about birth control, so they rarely use protection.[20]

You may be thinking, "Thank you very much, but I didn't really need to know about all that. I just want to keep my mom comfortably housed and well fed." I understand. Just be aware of the possibilities. After all, when seniors are determined to live with a lot of heart, romance can be part of the picture.

Chapter 10

❦

CELEBRATING OLD SOULS

*He makes me lie down in green pastures, he leads me beside quiet
waters, he restores my soul.*

—Psalm 23:2–3

I was staying at my sister's on this visit, and I was frustrated with
myself for not leaving enough time to get across town to go to
Sunday services with my mom in her assisted living community. At
least five minutes late, I walked into her apartment to find her sitting
at her little kitchen table waiting for me—all dressed up in her Sunday
best even though we were only going to take the elevator up to the
second floor of her building.

"You're late! Let's go!" she said, hopping up as fast as she could.
As we walked off the elevator onto the second floor, I understood
why she didn't want to miss a moment of the service. The group,
about thirty in number, were seated in folding chairs arranged in
rows. They were already singing the first hymn, but a friend of

Mom's who knew I was coming with her that day had saved us two seats, so we slipped in easily. Soon our voices were also lifted up in praise.

I had been concerned for some time that my mom didn't want to return to her home church across town after moving into assisted living. My sisters would offer to pick her up and take her, but she'd just casually dismiss the idea. That Sunday I understood. Her neighborhood Presbyterian church was full of memories of my dad and of all the years she had served there in church circles. A few old friends were left, but Cecil wasn't alive to sit with her anymore, and there were now more "ghosts" in the pews than living people Mom knew. This group at her facility was her community of faith now—people she ate with, played bridge with, and shared jokes with during the week. To top it off, the volunteer pastor was a Baptist, revitalizing my mom with some of the old hymns and solid Bible teaching of her youth. Here was her church, one floor closer to heaven, and she loved everything about it. By the time the service ended, so did I.

Many years before, the Lord had placed on my heart a desire to connect older adults with their faith—or introduce them for the first time to Jesus Christ and the blessed assurance of eternal life that could be theirs. It all started in 1999 at a book group meeting, where I overheard one friend ask another if she would consider facilitating a Bible study at an assisted living facility. No, said the other woman, she didn't have time. I felt the Holy Spirit tapping my shoulder and saying, "That invitation was supposed to be for you." So a few days later, I contacted the facility and began a weekly Bible study with a fascinating group of residents.

After about a year, I realized I needed to devote more time to helping my mother-in-law and mom, so I stopped going, but by then the Lord had planted in my heart and mind the idea for devotional lessons directed to the aging population. I began working on the project as I had time, calling it *The Hope of Glory* after the verse in Colossians

1:27: "Christ in you, the hope of glory." I tried shopping it around to publishers but didn't get an acceptance, so it just joined other back-burner projects in my files.

But the Holy Spirit didn't forget about it. In May 2010, I began visiting my friend Denise in the assisted living facility she had just moved into. At first it was difficult for me to even enter the building, as it brought back so many memories of my mother-in-law and my mom, both of whom had now passed away. But I kept going back because of Denise, and I began to feel more comfortable there. One day I stopped to look at the activities calendar posted on the wall. I noticed there were no Bible studies listed. The Holy Spirit used that information to get my attention again.

My church is almost across the street from the assisted living facility. A few days later, as I was leaving it, I heard the Spirit say, "Why don't you just go over there and ask them if they need you?" So I did. I walked into the activities director's office, introduced myself, told her where I went to church, and said, "Do you need someone to lead a Bible study or anything?" She smiled and said, "I left my card at your church, but I haven't heard from anyone yet." I got chills as we both realized God had sent me. I had my assignment.

Just weeks later, I began volunteering, writing a new lesson for the class each week. Once I had fifty-two lessons plus five more for special holidays, I began the search for a publisher again. *The Hope of Glory: A Devotional Guide for Older Adults* was released in March 2014. I'm not telling you all this to promote the book (although I'd love for you to see what it has to offer the seniors you know and love), but to reassure you that God has not forgotten the oldsters among us. His heart burns with love for them, and He sends His people to minister to them and share the life-saving truth of the gospel with them.

So many older people have rejected God because of tragedies and disappointments. Others are still sitting on the fence, never committing their lives to the Lord. They are running out of time. The time is now to lead them into a fuller understanding of God's eternal plan for them. That's my passion, and I pray it will be yours as you minister to the seniors you love.

Reaching Out

Should you decide the best way to reach your loved one may be to volunteer to lead a group yourself, be prepared for one of the most humbling ministries you'll ever experience. The first challenge is rounding up people to attend—and yet I've learned that allowing time to visit in each room as I gather residents or take them back after class is so important. That's when I have a chance to visit, see their photos, and learn about their lives.

Several times I've found a regular attendee, Sally, and gotten her settled in the activities room only to come back with another resident a few minutes later and realize Sally is gone. She truly loves to come and participates each week, but it's hard to keep her focused. There are a lot of sweet Sallys.

Another challenge is physically getting all the wheelchairs, walkers, and canes situated so you can begin. But don't let this or anything else discourage you from volunteering, because the rewards are great. Some days I leave thinking, "Well, I don't know if anyone got anything out of that lesson or not, but at least they weren't in their rooms watching *The Price Is Right*." Other days I've had residents say sweet things in response to the class. Betty said, "You know, we're here all the time. We could get together and talk about God any time we want to, but we don't unless you come. Thank you for coming." Similarly, one day Mary said, "Thank you for coming to encourage us to think about Jesus." I love hearing the attendees laugh together or seeing one weathered hand reach out to grasp another. Those are the kinds of bonuses that keep volunteers committed.

If the residence where your loved one lives does not have a Bible study or devotional hour on the schedule and you're not able to start one, ask if there is a visiting chaplain. If so, arrange to introduce him or her to your loved one. Where I volunteer, Rex is the chaplain who makes the rounds. He's an outgoing, caring fellow, so the ladies brighten up when they know he's in the building. And they do know, because he sings hymns at the top of his voice. He also spends quiet times in discussion and prayer with individual residents and has led several of them into life-changing relationships with the Lord.

I've learned I'm not alone in my passion for wanting every older person to tap into a life of faith. The Lord has called many to reach out to the elderly. Missy Buchanan, author of the book *My Story, My Song* with Robin Roberts and Lucimarian Roberts, has written several books dealing with aging and faith. She speaks across the country encouraging people to include an emphasis on faith in their care plan for the elderly. "Sometimes you just know when you've experienced a holy nudge," she says of her own calling. "A stirring of your soul that moves you in a certain direction. For me, the nudge has moved me to reach out to older adults, especially those who are struggling to find purpose and who need a dose of spiritual encouragement."[1]

It's difficult for anyone to find purpose without faith, and that's especially true for the aged. Those who believe God still has them on this earth for a reason can get up and get dressed each day anticipating how God will use them. During the day they never hesitate to give someone a smile, pat a hand, share a dessert, or crack a joke. They know that these simple acts of kindness have mighty purpose. They go to bed and sleep well, knowing that if they should die before they wake, they will wake up in heaven!

Whatever belief system has sustained seniors throughout their lives, if they had one, is critical to their well-being now. I respect the need of some elders to find comfort in the Jewish faith of their youth, or whatever religion they embraced. Of course I also want to gently introduce them to Jesus so He can give them the blessed assurance of eternal life.

I've observed that doctrinal differences have a way of becoming less important the older we grow. Within our group in assisted living are former Lutherans, Methodists, Catholics, and more. The Catholics make a point of also receiving communion from a Eucharistic minister once a week, but they have no problem talking about the Lord with us Protestants. In his wonderful book *Answering God*, Eugene Peterson writes this about such liturgical community: "God wants us outside the walls that quarantine us in our ego-sickness; he pulls us into the great dance of grace in which we find ourselves moving rhythmically and joyfully with partner after partner."[2] At a certain point in life, you realize that those who accept Jesus Christ as Lord and Savior are all going to be in heaven together, so we might as well learn to get along now. Preferences and doctrines fall away like jackets on a warm afternoon, leaving such essentials of the Christian faith as the deity of Jesus, the Word of God, prayer, and the fellowship of believers.

Regular weekly devotional hours are a wonderful way to introduce more spirituality into the routine of skilled nursing or assisted living residences. There are other ways besides. One-on-one visits with prayer time together soothe the souls of both the one who pays the visit and the one who receives it. Holding weekly church services in facilities, leading hymn and praise sing-alongs, or providing transportation so that residents can still attend their preferred place of worship also meet the need.

What does all this mean in the lives of your elders? How will this season of life be easier or fuller if their souls are nurtured? In as many ways as there are stars in the sky. Most significantly, what I notice in the faith-centered elders I encounter is a positive difference in their attitudes, in their ability to fight off the temptation to complain or withdraw, in their ability to forgive themselves and others, and in the way they are able to process grief.

Dr. Richard Johnson, a psychologist, author, and pioneer in spiritual aging, undertook a four-year research project that found fifty factors distinguishing positive from negative aging. Boiling it all down, he said that the main difference is faith. "The later years are essentially a spiritual journey. Certainly there are physical aspects to it, emotional aspects to it, psychological aspects to it, which all have to be attended to. But if that spiritual component is missing, then aging becomes a very dismal thing. Because all we are looking at is the demise of the body."[3]

I love witnessing such life-changing faith in elders. When I read through the discussion questions included with the lessons in *The Hope of Glory*, I'm transported to the activities room where we hold the Bible study. I envision the dear older faces of those seated around that table, and I remember what they said in response to each question. "I'm looking forward to seeing my mother," said Mamie when asked what she anticipated about heaven. "Just look out the window! Look at the mountains, the trees, and the birds!" said Sara when asked how we know there is a God. "Because He's always with me," said Mary when asked how we can be sure Jesus cares for us.

Our seniors have lost so much. Almost daily another bodily function escapes their control, another relationship ends, or more worldly props are removed. But God never changes. "Jesus Christ is the same yesterday and today and forever" (Heb. 13:8). Once they have the assurance of eternal life, they can lift their heads and go through each day unafraid. When things happen that they don't understand, or when unsettling medical reports arrive, they can say with the psalmist in Psalm 31:14, "I trust in you, LORD; I say, 'You are my God.'" It makes a difference.

In chapter 6, I mentioned going to the memorial service of a dear friend in our church, Grandma T. As the service she had carefully planned came to a close, the pastor told us we would all be given a fork as we left. He explained that it was because Grandma T believed that, just as they always tell you to save your fork at church potlucks because dessert is coming, the best is yet to come when we die as well—so save your fork. I have my fork in my purse as a constant reminder that there's more to this life than what I see. The best is yet to come. That hope of glory is a great comfort to elders. It's a hope that will never disappoint, never fail.

Sharing Faith

Many of us find it easier to discuss living arrangements, medical care, and even the need to stop driving than to ask our parents what they believe. Most of the older generation who came to faith in God internalized their faith. They didn't think it necessary to tell everyone else what they believed. That's well and good. All that really matters is that God knows their hearts. Yet it adds to our own peace of mind and helps us know how to minister to them when we know where they are spiritually.

My mom would frequently refer to "the good Lord," and she went to church all her life. She led devotions in church circles and said grace before meals. Still, as it became obvious that she was drawing near the end of her life, I needed the blessed assurance that I would see her in heaven someday. Finally I got up the courage to ask her if she believed that Jesus was the Son of God, that He died for our sins, and that through faith in Him alone she would be with Him in heaven. I think she said something like, "Well, of course I do. Let's go to lunch." But it put my heart at rest. Later, I had more confirmation that she was with the Lord.

My mother-in-law was a faithful member of the Episcopal church all her life, serving on the altar guild. Again, she didn't talk about her faith, but she washed and ironed linens for the church week after week and made being in Bible studies a priority. The notes in her Bible assured us her faith was rock solid.

Now, when we sing the hymn "Holy, Holy, Holy" in church and come to the line, "All the saints adore Thee, casting down their golden crowns around the glassy sea,"[4] my eyes fill with tears because I envision my mom, my mother-in-law, and all the older friends I've lost praising God and glorifying Him. I'm so grateful. What a beautiful cloud of witnesses is waiting to welcome me some day.

If you are caring for older adults who know the Lord, don't hesitate to ask questions about their faith as you visit. Ask questions like, "How do you stay constant in your walk with the Lord?" or "Was there a time in your life when circumstances caused you to question your faith?" Ask, "What parts of your life did God have to prune away in order to bring you closer to Him?" And, "What is your favorite Scripture verse and why?" Not only will you have a sweet time of sharing with your elder, one that blesses you both, but your own faith will be strengthened.

If your loved one doesn't have a personal faith, or if you're not sure what it is, don't hesitate to gently ask, "Have you thought about where you will go when you die?" or "Where is God in your life today?" The time for worrying about ruffling feathers is over. The time you have left with your parent is precious. Make the most of it. God will honor and bless any effort you make.

Dealing with Grief

A solid faith helps greatly when an older person suffers a significant loss. Not only may an elderly woman lose her husband, but she may lose an adult child as well. The grief would be unbearable without the hope of glory.

"The widow who is really in need and left all alone puts her hope in God and continues night and day to pray and to ask God for help," reads 1 Timothy 5:5.

My friend Lily knew the grief of losing a son. As we went around the table asking for prayer requests, she would say, "For Peter in heaven." Theologically speaking, I wasn't sure Peter still needed our prayers if he was in heaven, but I gladly added her request to the list.

Jesse, one of the centenarians in the ABC *20/20* show "100 and Still Growing," and his eighty-five-year-old wife, Phronie, had suffered many losses. Yet they went to church twice every week, and he, like many of the centenarians, believed his deep religious faith kept him going. When the researchers asked him if he was born again, Jesse responded, "Yes, sir. I know I've been born again. My hands look new. My feet look new. Yeah, He changed my heart. I had a hard heart, but He changed it." The researchers cite Jesse as an example of elders who thrive because of "the importance of being passionately involved in something you care about."[5] Yep, faith will do that for a person.

We can learn much about how to deal with grief by watching how older adults handle loss. While no one wants to experience grief, believers in Jesus Christ know that seasons of grief can be a blessing if they bring us closer to Him and make us more aware of our dependence on Him for lasting comfort. In that sense, our suffering produces "good grief" that God uses to grow our faith in Him.

If you need professional insight to help elders who are grieving, grief counselors frequently turn to *The Grief Recovery Handbook* by John W. James and Russell Friedman, founders of The Grief Recovery Institute, for guidance. The authors list the following common responses to grief: reduced concentration, a sense of numbness, disrupted sleep patterns, changed eating habits, and a roller coaster of emotional energy.[6]

Yet those who grieve as believers in Jesus Christ have a distinct advantage: they have the Lord of the Universe as their close companion. In times of despair, believers often express that they feel the power of the Lord sustaining them and helping them get through the painful details of their loss. Eventually, they experience the comfort and healing that only the Lord can provide.

Walking through grief with an older adult you love is one of the kindest gifts you can give. We cannot spare our elders their pain, nor can we escape periods of grief ourselves, but we can all rest in the knowledge that we will never have to go through grief alone. And the time is coming when we will never have to grieve again, for we will be with the Lord in heaven, where He promises to wipe away our tears. The greatest comfort we can offer is God's comfort—comfort that is based on an eternal perspective.

A Life of Faith

Having a life of faith not only sustains us as we age, but it also fills us with passion. Being dedicated to serving the Lord, and following

His direction in our lives, is a passion from which people never seem to retire.

My husband and I stay in touch with a favorite pastor from years past, Ron Ritchie. In a recent newsletter from Ron's ministry, Free at Last!, he writes about his involvement in a team-approach training program for four young Christian interns: "I was asked to lead them into the study of the New Covenant as found in 2 Corinthians 1–6. My teaching, every Tuesday morning for eight weeks, was done over the Skype video network. It was a delight to be part of that team."[7]

Ron recently turned eighty. He describes his wife, Anne Marie, also up in years, as his "techie" on the Skype teaching. They are partners in life and ministry—so close that Ron signs all his correspondence with one word: RonAnneMarie. They experience joy and fulfillment not because they've avoided difficulties and disappointments in life but because they cling to the promises of God. They are blessed with purpose and passion, all because of Him.

As this book was about to go to print, I learned that a dear old friend of mine, Dorothy, had gone to be with the Lord. Dorothy cleaned house for us every other week for over twenty-five years. Often she would knock on my home office door to ask me if I had time to chat. Whether I did or didn't, I always made time for Dorothy. We circled many topics in our chats, but always returned to our mutual trust in the Lord. The last time I saw Dorothy, after she was forced to stop working because the doctor put her on oxygen, she came by the house to pick up six of my books to use in a Bible study she planned to lead at the senior apartment complex where she lived. Dorothy was the embodiment of Colossians 3:23: "Whatever you do, work at it with all your heart, as working for the Lord." Dorothy lived a life of faith.

The job of all of us who care for the old souls we love is to encourage them to seek this same life of faith: to believe in the One who offers them eternal life, and to rest in the knowledge that they are never alone, for He is with them—even when we can't be.

Chapter 11

TAKING CARE

Therefore encourage one another and build each other up,
just as in fact you are doing.

—1 Thessalonians 5:11

At a dinner table of ten people, I found myself seated next to Ginny, an exhausted-looking woman several years younger than I. When another diner asked whether she would be accompanying her husband on a trip, I overheard her reply. "No," Ginny said, "since my mother lives with us."

My antennae are always up when it comes to aging parents, so during a lull in the conversation, I asked Ginny to tell me more about her mother. I did not know Ginny well, having only met her once before, but I was sincerely interested, and she desperately needed to share. What I heard was heartbreaking. Due to a stroke, her mother can't speak. She broke a shoulder during a fall, but for some reason it couldn't be set, so she is in constant pain. And on top of it all, she has dementia.

This has been the situation for five long, difficult years. Every day, all day. And every night.

Listening to Ginny's story, I realized anew how vast and varied is the role of caregiver to the aged. This woman is in the trenches. She has moved her office to her home in order to continue selling real estate. She doesn't visit her grandchildren in another state because she hasn't found reliable substitute care for her mom. And she doesn't travel with her husband for the same reason.

My caregiving experiences were a walk in the park compared to hers. True, I had a more hands-on role in caring for my mother-in-law than for my mother. But while Mary Frances was always on our minds during the years she needed extra care, and we jumped a bit whenever the telephone rang, my husband and I could still maintain a life of our own.

My caregiving for my own mom was long-distance. That created its own difficulties, but because Mom was many miles away and my sisters were there with her, her care wasn't part of my everyday responsibilities. So with her too, my life was only sporadically affected.

Not true for people like my dinner confidante. Those who haven't faced the kinds of decisions Ginny has made might quickly conclude that this is a person with a martyr complex. Someone who doesn't know about establishing healthy boundaries. Someone who, rather than controlling situations, lets situations control her. But that's just not so. Ginny's caregiving choices aren't based on limited resources either, but on unlimited love.

She's not alone. According to a study sponsored by AARP and the National Alliance of Caregiving, 43.4 million Americans ages eighteen and older provide some type of unpaid care to an adult age fifty and over. The average caregiver is a fifty-year-old woman who spends an average of nineteen hours every week caring for her mother. Up to 55 percent are also employed. The value of family caregiving to society is estimated at over $250 billion annually, but this dollar amount doesn't take into account the considerable physical and emotional toll exacted on caregivers.[1] And there's a disturbing trend moving forward: more people needing care and fewer people to provide it.

Of the caregivers interviewed for the study, those with the heaviest caregiving responsibilities report experiencing the highest levels of emotional stress, physical strain, and financial hardship. They say they cope by praying, turning to a friend or relative for advice, or searching for help in books or other materials.[2] Still, burnout is a real possibility for any caregiver. Once it becomes apparent that more help is needed, caregivers may turn to siblings, spouses, pastors, or professionals for support. In short, it's too much for one person to bear alone. You need help, so ask for it.

Siblings as Partners

Whether or not siblings work well together in caring for an aging parent hinges not only on their common love for the parent but also on their ability to communicate with one another.

My periodic visits to see my mom could only provide me with snapshots of her overall condition. But just as time lapse photography exposes change over time, my snapshot visits also exposed changes that were less obvious to those who saw my mother more frequently. I learned to repeatedly acknowledge my sisters for the selfless amount of time they spent with our mother, meeting her every need, taking her to all her doctor appointments, and so forth. In turn, they eventually learned to value my snapshot perspective. Only when we combined our experiences and insights did we see a clear picture of Mom's situation developing.

Friends of mine who are only children often long for someone to share the burden of caring for their aging parent, while those with siblings sometimes feel things would be so much simpler if they could just make all the decisions without having to run them by a belligerent brother or self-centered sister. But the job of caring for an aging parent is too big and too exhausting for one person. Most who have siblings ultimately realize that to ignore the obvious resources for help and support would be not only unwise but also self-destructive.

Jane Gross, writing in *A Bittersweet Season,* is very open about her relationship with her brother as they cared for their aging mom. "As time passed," she writes, "Michael and I both became increasingly frayed, with the situation in general and with the unfamiliar experience of being yoked to each other."[3] Not particularly close as adults, Jane and Michael eventually agreed on a division of labor that seemed mostly equitable, although Jane did have her moments when she realized her duties involved changing her mother's adult diapers and his involved writing checks. They also disagreed about whether it was acceptable for both of them to be out of town at the same time once their mom was moved into a care center. Ultimately, they worked out their differences and became much closer in the process. Their functioning partnership no doubt brought their mother more comfort than anything else they could have done for her.

My friend Gail reflects on her experience with her brother a bit differently. "I could not possibly have gone through this experience without my brother. He and I both lived far away from our parents, so we took turns visiting them, maintaining their home, setting up in-home services, and talking to doctors. It was such a relief to share the burden—and the tears and the laughter too."

More often one adult child is present in the same town with the aging parent and, if only for geographic reasons, has to take the lead. "My brother and sister live hours away so their only involvement was to visit my mom occasionally and to validate my actions. I kept them informed," said another friend, Bruce.

Like Gail and Bruce, my husband and I were blessed to have solid, loving, working relationships with our siblings while caring for our moms. But I know that's not the case for all caregivers. If the situation becomes untenable and is affecting the care of the aging parent, then it may be necessary to turn to eldercare mediation.

Missy Buchanan writes about one such sibling scenario. A middle-aged woman is frustrated that, once again, her brother has dropped in to visit their ailing mom over the holidays, bringing gifts and temporary attention but no plans to enter into the long-term caregiving responsibilities.

"She wasn't surprised when he started reciting his usual list of excuses," Missy writes. "She had heard them all before. He lives over a hundred miles away. He is self-employed and can't afford to be away from work. He has two teenagers to support and money is tight. He is just not emotionally equipped to handle watching their mother decline."[4] But where does that leave the sister? It leaves her with tears spilling down onto her Christmas sweater as she thinks about the energy, time, and money she has already spent caring for their mother.

In the same article, Missy introduces us to Keith Branson, founder of Age to Age Ministry and a conflict resolution specialist, who suggests that eldercare mediation offers the best hope in highly charged situations. A skillful mediator familiar with eldercare issues can help defuse the emotional tension and help everyone to see things more objectively. He can reframe the conversation with less antagonistic rhetoric than occurs when angry or hurt family members tackle the conversation alone, and he can help each party hear what the other is saying without judging or condemning. Branson also recommends that, unless aging parents are mentally unable to share in the decision-making, they be invited to join the conversation at the appropriate time.[5]

Aging centers in your community may be able to offer mediation services or refer you to another reliable source. You could consider hiring a family therapist, a geriatric care manager (www.caremanager.org), or a mediator who specializes in the elderly (www.mediate.com). If you are the caregiving sibling and get no support from your brothers or sisters, it's worth finding a way to get them on board—and the sooner the better. If all of you believe in the power of prayer, begin by praying together. Then the Holy Spirit will be your mediator. If you don't take the time and find a way to build consensus and work together, your aging parent will suffer, and so will you.

Spouses as Partners

Within our circle of friends are two outstanding examples of spouses who support one another in caregiving roles. Ross and Sue are the first couple. Sue's mom, Lois, sold her home to "the kids" but then built a guest house on the property where she lived for twenty years before moving into assisted living. Lois is a dear person, but I was always amazed by how attentive her son-in-law, Ross, was to her every need—including agreeing to a game of three-handed bridge night after night. As her mother aged, Sue's caregiver role grew more constant and draining, and she simply couldn't have made it without Ross.

Another couple we know, Mark and Pat, had a similar situation. Pat's mother, Mattie, lived in their home for more than twenty-five years. Early on, she was a great help in watching their three daughters and beginning meal preparations, but the older she got, the more care she required and the less she remembered. Still, Mark did everything necessary to help his mother-in-law age in place and his wife keep her sanity.

Ross and Mark were both available for doctor appointments and the occasional ER run, making it possible for their wives to care for their mothers without totally abandoning their own lives.

My husband, Jim, so appreciated everything I did for his mother that it was easy for him to support my efforts to care for my own mother at the same time. Since we were in Colorado and she was in Tennessee, this usually meant I traveled alone to see Mom while Jim stayed home to work and take care of his own mother. We always laughed when my mom would say, "Tell Jim I said thank you for letting you come." He was pretty sure wild horses wouldn't have been able to keep me away.

Yet caregiving can cause stress in a marriage. For Debra, the hardest part of caring for her dad in her home was the arguments with her husband. "He felt my dad was being ornery deliberately," she said, "yet I knew he just didn't understand what he was doing or saying anymore."

If your husband or wife isn't as supportive and helpful as you had hoped, have you told your spouse how very much he or she is needed? There are times when you only need to be held while you cry, but you need that so very much. Spouses who are not the biological children of the older adults needing help can often look at each situation far more objectively and help the caregiver put hysteria and chaos in perspective. In the best of cases, they may also be able to mediate between siblings to some degree. Don't go looking for help outside of your home until you've exhausted all the resources within it. Tell your spouse specifically how he or she can help; then step aside and let him or her do what you've asked—even if it's not exactly the way you would do it.

When Friends Are Caregivers

Younger or more able-bodied friends of the very old can also be a huge help to overwhelmed caregivers. I always worry a bit when I see one aged driver picking up a car full of other older adults, but if you know your parent's friend is capable of driving and she offers to help, say yes.

Maybe the help you need doesn't involve transportation. You just need someone to check in on your mom on days when you can't. Ask a friend of hers to do so.

Older adults get tired of being a burden on their adult children, and frankly, they can use a break from us too. Help from a longtime friend can be a welcome relief for them and maybe more fun—especially if a joint activity or card game is part of the plan.

In New York City, there is a group with a more formalized approach to peer support. Members of the Caring Collaborative—a program offering volunteer assistance to women with health problems—meet in neighborhood groups, organized by ZIP code, for confidential discussions of doctors, hospitals, and surgical procedures. They also help one another with things like a ride home from the eye doctor or from a colonoscopy, and with tasks such as dog-walking.[6]

In suburban neighborhoods across America, caring neighbors often help their aging neighbors, and frequently they have a more accurate picture of how the older adult is doing than the elder's own family.

My friend Pat and her family moved into a house next to a very nice older couple thirty-plus years ago. They were cordial neighbors all those years, but after the husband died, Pat and her spouse began doing more and more tasks for the aging widow.

"I put the newspaper on her front porch every morning," Pat remembers. "If she hadn't picked it up by midday, I would call. If she didn't answer, I would leave a message telling her I was coming over to check on her. Luckily, she was usually just involved in something or away from the phone. However, I always worried about what I would find."

This woman had adult children, but they lived out of town, and she did a good job of convincing them all was well whenever they called to check on her. If she ever expressed the slightest concern to them, however, they would overreact and call 911, resulting in many unnecessary and expensive trips to the ER over the years. Finally a bad fall sent her to the hospital to stay, and her family had to step in and take control. They eventually moved her into assisted living in another state.

Pat was sad to lose her longtime neighbor and friend, but at the same time relieved, because she realized that she had slowly taken on responsibilities that took her from good neighbor status to caregiver. She had also been somewhat apprehensive that the family might hold her responsible for anything that happened. The lesson here is that you should consider neighbors who want to help a valuable resource, but let them be part of a team of caregivers meeting an elder's needs, not the sole support.

Churches too can be part of the caregiving team, and they actually have that responsibility. James 1:27 reads, "Religion that God our Father accepts as pure and faultless is this: to look after orphans and widows in their distress." Certainly looking after older men who are alone is the Christian thing to do also. Many churches have visitation teams and prayer teams who would be happy to include your aging parent as a recipient of their visits or prayers—and the elderly need both. If your loved one was active in a church, do all you can to keep the connection alive, even if Sunday attendance is not possible. If your parent was not part of a church fellowship in the past, perhaps a neighborhood church would like to know that an older person nearby could use their support. Make the phone call.

A caregiver needs to set pride aside and ask for help from as many sources as possible. At worst, someone will say, "I'm sorry. I don't think I'll be able to do that." Then you say, "Thank you for considering it," and move on to the next option.

Some of us volunteer to be caregivers, and some of us reluctantly fill the role because there's no one else. None of us knows everything we need to know going in. Nancy L. Snyderman, MD, is the chief medical editor for *NBC News*, yet even she was caught off guard. "It would be easy to assume that, as a doctor, I could navigate the health care system with ease. But I was as overwhelmed as the next person," she said about caring for her parents in their late eighties. "My medical expertise just fueled my exasperation. . . . Perhaps the most important lesson I learned in all of this is how little we plan for the inevitable crises—and how much we all need help."[7]

Sometimes that help comes from friends of the caregivers. "My husband and I didn't understand how bad things were getting until we had some good friends sit us down and talk about how stressed we seemed," said Julie, my friend caring for her grandmother. "If they hadn't been willing to intervene, we may not have gotten her the care she truly needed in time."

When You're the Bologna

As difficult as it is to care for aging parents, my heart especially goes out to those who are rearing children at the same time. Those who have both adult diapers and acne medicine on their grocery list.

Those who must decide between a program at the high school or meeting the ambulance carrying their aging parent to the ER—again.

Known as the "sandwich generation," these people have many days when they are pressed from both sides. They are in the difficult middle; they are the bologna. For them, it is caregiving times two.

For Evelyn Volk of Los Angeles, mornings begin with rustling her two teenage kids out of bed for school and then checking on her elderly mother, who suffers from dementia and lives with the family.

"On a good day, I feel like Superwoman," she said. But other days, many of the items on her to-do list are not checked off when she falls into bed. Sometimes it's hard for her to focus during the day because she gets easily sidetracked. "Everything takes so much out of me," she says. "I don't like those days."

Roughly a third of Americans who take care of a parent, spouse, relative, or other loved one are rearing children as well, according to the nonprofit National Alliance for Caregiving. "They're struggling to find a balance," said Gail Hunt, who heads this group. "They feel guilty that they're not doing enough no matter how much they do."[8]

Several factors contribute to the increasing number of people drafted into double-duty caregiving. For many, the recent recession has made other options unattainable. Also, women are having children later in life. And the elderly are living longer. No wonder the sandwich generation is expanding.

One advantage to having your children at a relatively young age is that they are mostly reared and on their own before you must turn your attention to your aging parents. My husband and I enjoyed a period of more than ten years between when our last child left for college and the first of our mothers needed more of our help. During that time, we enjoyed visits with our adult children, our grandkids, and our aging parents, but no one needed our constant care.

The closest I came to experiencing the stress of the sandwich generation was the summer my mother was dying in Tennessee. I had long before agreed to keep my son's three children while he and his wife led a mission trip to Kenya. These were the grandchildren I didn't get to see very often, so I was looking forward to having them all to ourselves for almost three weeks. As the time approached, it became obvious my mother was not doing well. Yet my sisters assured me they had things well in hand, and I should continue with the babysitting plans.

But once the children were here with us, and their parents, Tim and Abigail, were on another continent, my mother entered hospice care. Much as I wanted to be in the moment with Ellie, Jack, and Peter, I felt compelled to answer the phone each time one of my sisters called—and they called often, because hard decisions were being made, and they wanted me to feel a part of all that was happening to our mom.

What this limited experience taught me is that caregivers who are pulled in two directions are likely to be more distracted, feel more anxious, and sleep even less than those without the double duty. It's so important for those who are in the sandwich generation long-term to be part of a strong support group, to get respite from time to time, and to enlist the help of others when possible.

No parents want to overburden their children with caring for their grandparents, but on the other hand, children learn compassion when they can help with simple tasks within their ability. They also develop a deeper understanding of what it means to grow older—an understanding that will serve them well as they move into your role someday, and as they themselves age. Be specific with older children in a multigenerational household about what they can do to help. It may be something simple like, "Please sit and watch TV with Grandma while I run to the store." Or, "Please remind Grandpa to take his pills at 3:00 PM." Tell them how their help makes it possible for you to spend more time with them.

Similarly, if aging parents in your home are still able to help with simple preparations for dinner, fold laundry, or play a game with a cranky grandchild, then ask for that help. It will restore your sanity and their sense of purpose.

Taking Care of Finances

You may have a power of attorney to help with your aging parent's finances, or you may find that you have backed into that role without ever agreeing to accept it. My mother-in-law had macular degeneration, and it became harder and harder for her to balance her checkbook, see where to sign her name on checks and other documents, etc. Fortunately, she had designated my husband to exercise financial power of attorney on her behalf, and he did a wonderful job helping her keep up with her finances.

We still laugh about one aspect of their financial agreement. Jim paid the bills for Mary Frances, but she liked to have a few checks on hand for service providers, such as the wonderful hairdresser who came to her house to do her hair. These were people Mary Frances could trust to fill out the amount she specified and show her exactly where to sign. Occasionally we would come home to find a message from Jim's mom—who never felt comfortable using voicemail—saying, "Jim, I need checks." Click.

Experts agree that it's extremely important to keep accurate records of all financial transactions that you, as the financial caregiver, manage, and to keep all these records, and all accounts, separate from your own. This can be extremely important when it comes to paying taxes, settling estates, and so forth. If you have siblings, it's also a good idea to send a report to everyone at least once a quarter, clearly delineating income and expenses. It's also advisable to include your siblings in major financial decisions. "Doing otherwise can breed suspicion," says Harry Margolis, an elder-law attorney at Margolis & Bloom LLP in Boston.[9]

Everything my husband did to take care of his mother's finances was voluntary, as was the same service my older sister provided to our mom. But eldercare attorneys and mediators may sometimes recommend that the primary caregiver should be compensated in some way, especially if that person handles finances. Once this decision is made, Margolis says, the family should document the caregiver's responsibilities, hours, and pay in a formal contract and disclose the arrangements to everyone in the family.

If the parent may need to rely on Medicaid to cover future nursing home costs, the family should consult an elder-law attorney about how to avoid the appearance of trying to hide assets.[10] This can be complicated, but if finances are your responsibility, it's important to look ahead, assess present and future resources, and come up with a plan that, to the best of your ability to foresee future needs, will cover your parent's care.

When a caregiver has to give up a paying job in order to care for aging parents, any compensation the parents or family can provide is appropriate and needed. This was the case with AARP's Amy Goyer.

Amy traveled back and forth from Washington, DC, to Arizona many times over the twenty years after her mom's stroke. But when her dad developed Alzheimer's, the distance became problematic. "So I adapted my work, choosing jobs that let me telecommute, and began working from Arizona a week or two a month," Amy explained.[11]

When even that wasn't enough, Amy moved into her parents' home. Like many other caregivers who need to work at the same time they are caring for their aging parents, she had to find a compromise that allowed her to meet her job requirements and the needs of her parents.

If you find yourself in a similar position, don't hesitate to tell your boss. Be honest and realistic about your options. Change your work hours if that helps meet your caregiving demands, and consider telecommuting at least part-time. It may be possible to take an extended leave. There's no guarantee your job will be waiting for you once your caregiving duties are over, but if you qualify, ask your employer about the Family Medical Leave Act. And remember, even if you have to leave work for a while, this is only for a season.

"I've made a conscious choice to care for them . . . so I've adapted my work and career goals. People ask me how I do it," Amy writes. "I wonder, how could I not do it? I succeed because I want to and because I believe so strongly in what I'm doing."[12]

Caregiver Burnout

Being a caregiver to an older adult, especially one you love and have known and relied upon all your life, is a tough assignment. No sugar-coating here. Those who get thrown into the midst of caregiving without the luxury of planning in advance, researching options, and lining up resources are the most likely to suffer the devastating effects of caregiver burnout. Frequent symptoms can include denial, anger, social withdrawal, anxiety, depression, exhaustion, sleeplessness, irritability, lack of concentration, and health problems.

In an article titled "The Quiet Crisis" for the *Atlantic*, Jonathan Rauch described his desperation in trying to take care of his aging father. Readers coast to coast no doubt echoed their "me toos!" into the heavens. Jonathan moved his father into an apartment near him in Washington, DC, but things did not go well.

After an incident at Costco when his father went stiff on one side, was unable to stand, and didn't know where he was, Jonathan wrote, "That was the day I realized that he could not cope, and I could not cope, and, emotionally, he could take me down with him."[13]

Rauch reports that, according to the Rosalynn Carter Institute for Caregiving at Georgia Southwestern State University (an excellent resource), family caregivers face elevated risks to their physical health, mental health, finances, employment, and retirement. Fortunately, when his father realized the toll that caregiving was taking on his son, he agreed to move to an assisted living facility. Rauch said, "He was still, after all, my father, and it was still his job to take care of me."[14]

"I emerged from the experience not a little indignant," Jonathan writes of his own recovery afterwards. "The medical infrastructure for elder care in America is good, very good. But the cultural infrastructure is all but nonexistent. How can it be that so many people like me are so completely unprepared for what is, after all, one of life's near certainties?"[15] That may be one of the most perplexing questions of our generation.

Caregivers I've talked to expressed the challenges and frustrations of their role in many different ways. Although most are women, many men take on the role of caregiver and may have to work through a tendency to want to quickly "fix" things. Some things can't be fixed.

Yvette, a caregiver, reinforces the importance of empathy: "Change is extremely hard at any age, but it is much harder for the elderly, so it is important to keep that in mind and to consider what they are experiencing, even when the caregivers are stressed and tired."

Celia Watson Seupel had rearranged her life to take in her elderly mother, setting up a home office so that she could schedule activities and side trips with her mom as needed. The arrangement was working beautifully until one day it suddenly seemed unbearable.

"Why all of a sudden did I feel as if I didn't love my mother, that I hated taking care of her?" she cried out.

"What you're describing is really a matter of resentment," said Barry J. Jacobs, psychologist and author of *The Emotional Survival Guide for Caregivers*. "Sometimes caregivers have a difficult time distinguishing between resenting the caregiving and resenting the person. It's a clear sign of burnout."[16]

Celia came to realize that over time she had set aside a lot of her usual activities: taking long walks, going out with friends, even her morning spiritual quiet times. She worked to restore these nurturing activities into her schedule, and warm, loving feelings toward her mother returned.

"The experts say that caregivers must make time for themselves, but what I realized is how important the quality of that time is," she writes. "Time for oneself doesn't mean time working alone, even when it's work I love. It means taking time off to connect with friends, to have fun and for me, most importantly, to renew from a wellspring deeper than my own."[17]

In closing this chapter, I encourage you not to do another thing until you visit A Caregiver's Bill of Rights online and post a copy of it where you can see it several times a day.[18] You are doing mighty, holy work. Take care of yourself.

Chapter 12

HOLDING HANDS ACROSS THE MILES

*May the LORD keep watch between you and me when we are
away from each other.*

—Genesis 31:49

You see them in every airport. They are the ones with one roller bag by their feet and two bags under their eyes. The ones with furrowed brows as they answer a ringing cell phone. They can't remember the last time they took a trip for fun instead of out of commitment and guilt, so try not to flaunt your tan or admire the cell phone photos you took at the beach while sitting next to them in the airport lounge. They are the roller bag brigade of Baby Boomers flying to care for aging parents.

Once our society became so mobile, it was inevitable that distance between older parents and the adult children who love them would become more problematic. Sometimes it's the kids who move, following the lure of a job, a relationship, or an adventure. But it may also be the parents who move in search of a climate not requiring hats, mittens, and snow shovels. Regardless, the older and more infirm parents become, the more difficult the distance becomes as well. It's one thing to worry about your mom who lives alone in her own home nearby, down the hall in your guest room, or across town in assisted living. But when you can't just knock on the door or drop by to check on her, you may find yourself waking up in the middle of the night with more than a small amount of anxiety.

Long-distance caregivers who are only children bear the greatest burden. After years of trying to time trips to help their parents accomplish necessary transitions and tasks, it's understandable that they would propose that their parents move closer to them. Yet I've met many assisted living residents who miss the neighborhoods, churches, and friends they left behind just to be closer to their adult children, some of whom rarely have time to visit anyway.

An eldercare ombudsman who spoke to our gerontology class shared a case study in which a Baby Boomer couple announced they were going to move one of their moms out of a retirement community in Arizona to a facility in Colorado. "Why would you want to do that?" the advisor asked. "If she's doing well there, why would you want to remove her from her support group, her doctor, and her community?" What may be easier for the adult children may not be in the best interests of the aging parent. And so the difficult distance remains.

Most of the thirty-plus years I lived 1,305 miles away from my Tennessee mom worked out OK. I'm blessed to have two sisters who took very good care of her, leaving me to play the role of out-of-town daughter and welcome guest. Whenever I made plans to come to town, my mom would roll out the red carpet, enlisting my sisters to help her get everything prepared because "Nancy's coming." Thankfully, my sisters and I were able to laugh together about how they were supposed to drop everything to help Mom celebrate my arrival and entertain me. I think she saw me as a cross between the prodigal daughter for whom she should kill the fatted calf, and the lost sheep being welcomed back into the fold. Although she applauded the life I lived in Colorado and usually came to visit at least once a year for as long as she was able, I can't say she was ever truly at peace with my living "way out there."

Our last couple years of separation were the hardest for us both. As my mother's health began to fail, she couldn't visit me, so I doubled up on visits to her. The year before she died, I made six trips from Colorado Springs to Knoxville, Tennessee. That year, I definitely earned roller bag brigade status.

And I gained a heart of empathy for daughters and sons who don't have siblings living in the same town as their aging parents. When their parents need them so much, how can they manage while also meeting the demands of their jobs, families, and other responsibilities? How can they bear up under the financial strain brought on by so many flights—especially those ultra-expensive last-minute ones? The wisest seek help and accept it gladly.

Assessing from Afar

A familiar scenario plays out in kitchens and living rooms all over America. It's Sunday afternoon, and Mom and Dad receive a long-distance call from their dutiful son or daughter many miles away. Some in-town relatives have dropped by for a visit, so they are able to overhear Mom or Dad answering all the questions asked over the phone with variations of, "Just fine." The relatives' eyes roll as they assess the situation before them.

Because our parents are still our parents, they don't want to worry us. My mother often told my sisters not to bother me with news of her health issues because I was "way out there where I couldn't do anything about it anyway." There was some truth to that. I couldn't pick her up to take her to the doctor, but I could pray, and I did want to know what was going on. Her protection of me, while well-intentioned, resulted in my feeling left out. Yet when I did visit her, she would often communicate fears and concerns to me that she hadn't expressed to my sisters. Somehow I think she saw me as safe to confide in, because I was going to get on a plane for home and wouldn't be around to force her to do anything she didn't want to do.

So how can we break through the "I'm fine" barrier to find out how our aging parents are really doing? It's a challenge. Any skills you may have in getting information out of a teenager may need to come into play. For one thing, try to refrain from asking only yes or no questions. Rather than ask, "Did you eat supper?" ask, "What did you eat for supper?" If the answer is too often something like, "Raisins and a piece of toast," then you know nutrition may be a concern. When parents are aging in place, questions about home maintenance should also be specific. Rather than asking, "Is everything OK around the house?" maybe you say, "I saw on the weather report that you had quite a rain on Friday. Did you see any water coming into the house? Did the roof leak?"

Donna moved with her pastor husband to set up a ministry in New Zealand in the mid-1990s. Although the Internet wasn't nearly as widely used as it is today, Donna took the time to get a computer for her eighty-year-old dad and teach him to use it before leaving the country. "It took much patience and repetitive teaching, but it was also so rewarding to see him love it," Donna says. "It was the best thing I could have done because we could stay in touch face-to-face through Skype later. I would even help my dad with problems on his computer through Skype. Instead of just speaking to him on the phone, I could actually see his face and enjoy him as though I were there with him. It was really special."

Now we have not only Skype to stay in touch visually but also face time on smart phones. Not all octogenarians are as open to learning how to use these communication tools as Donna's dad (she called him "amazing"). However, it's certainly worth a try, because this is a case where a picture truly is worth a thousand words. You can learn a lot about an older adult's nutrition, hygiene, and general well-being through visual technology. You may even pick up clues about living conditions. If your parent won't learn to use Skype, maybe there's a ten-year-old neighbor you could hire to set it up each time.

It's important to build alliances with others of all ages who can give you an up close and personal assessment of how things are going. If you don't have a sibling to be your eyes and ears, is there a friend, relative, or neighbor you trust? When you have a particular concern, you can let that person know what to look for. Many people will gladly provide this service unpaid. But most long-distance caregivers would gladly compensate someone to play this role. It's far less expensive than a last-minute plane ticket.

Financial situations can be the most difficult to assess. In her book *Caring for Yourself While Caring for Your Aging Parents*, Claire Berman tells of Nate, a long-distance caregiver who enlisted the help of a trusted housekeeper. "She looks in on Mother and does the grocery shopping," Nate says. "I send her a check, she cashes it, and she sees that my mother has money. She's someone Mother trusts, and I do, too." When Nate visits his mother, he leaves the housekeeper a pile of self-addressed, stamped envelopes. "That way," he says, "when forms or bills arrive that may require my attention, she has simply to put them into one of the envelopes and mail them off to me. It's a simple idea, and it works."[1]

Horror stories are told of elderly residents having their electricity turned off because they either didn't have the funds to pay the bill or they forgot to do it. A neglected tax bill forced a senior in our community out of a home she'd lived in for thirty years—a home that was mortgage-free. Such misunderstandings can and should be corrected, but they can be difficult to manage from a distance.

Helping from a Distance

Technology not only can make it easier to communicate with distant parents, but it can also be our best friend when it comes to finding help for any number of needs. Thanks to search engines like Google and Bing, you can shop for care providers, read references, and uncover any concerns, all from your own home office. (The recommended resources at the back of the book can help get you started.)

Eldercare Locator is a nationwide service administered by the National Association of Area Agencies on Aging to help families learn about resources for older people in their community—services such as transportation, home-delivered meals, legal assistance, housing options, recreation and social activities, adult daycare, senior center programs, home health services, adult abuse prevention, and nursing homes. You may also access information at www.aoa.gov and then look for what you need.

You are already emotionally involved in caring for your parent from afar, but it's equally important for you to be *mentally* on board. Make up your mind that you are in this for the long haul. Ideally, being a long-distance caregiver is a part-time job, but it has the potential to morph into a full-time job with overtime. Accept this. Set up hardcopy files or computer files to help you stay on top of the aspects of care you are managing. Keep up-to-date records of doctor visits and conversations. Consider journaling—not only to help you keep facts straight, but also for the catharsis of pouring out your concerns and frustrations.

At minimum, you should have on file your parent's date of birth, social security number, Medicare or Medicaid number, and supplemental health plan information. Keep an up-to-date list of medications, complete with prescribed dosages, along with contact information for any doctors, clinics, or hospitals involved in his or her care. Having all this information at your fingertips will make it easier for you to take care of business from a distance even if you don't have power of attorney. (However, power of attorney is an important document to have in place the deeper you delve into caring for your elder.)

One word of caution: as long as your aging parent is mentally competent, remember to involve him or her in any decisions you must make. Don't dedicate an afternoon to checking off all the things you think need to be set in motion, yet forget to tell your dad that Meals on Wheels will begin meal service to him on Monday. The unsuspecting volunteer delivery person might not be warmly received! Adult children can often be more effective in gathering information and resources than their aging parents, but railroading through what they think is best without consulting their loved ones won't improve the quality of care or the parent-child relationship.

Making Trips Count

My friend Pat felt frustrated that her elderly neighbor's well-intentioned family didn't visit their mother more often. "Whenever they did come, it would be over a holiday or weekend when banks and doctors' offices were closed. It made me wonder if they came to help get things done for their mom or just to alleviate their own guilt." These adult children didn't go out of their way to talk to their mom's neighbors and local friends, and Pat wishes they had done so. "If more than one person says there is a problem, then there is a problem," she says. But they never asked, perhaps out of denial that their mom really did need more help.

If you are the only caregiver and a long-distance member of the roller bag brigade, advance planning is key to making each trip productive and mutually satisfying for you and your parent. Well in advance of your trip, set appointments with doctors, counselors, even neighbors and close friends you want to see with your parent while you are there. This doesn't guarantee a productive trip, but it certainly increases the odds.

Another key is to stay longer than a weekend. Talk to your employer and make other necessary arrangements for your trips so you can stay long enough to help with some of the many tasks that come with growing old—and still have some time left over to just *be* with your parent. If your mom is still living alone, put on your robe and slippers and just settle in with her in front of the television in the down time.

See what she proposes that the two of you have for dinner. Notice what time she goes to bed and gets up. This gives you a chance to observe the life she is really living, not the one she may pretend to be living if you are only in town for a couple of days.

If your dad lives in assisted living, see if you can stay in his apartment, even if it means losing sleep on an uncomfortable couch (as in my case). Again, you'll get an opportunity to observe real life. Is he climbing up on a stool to reach glasses that could be moved to a lower shelf? Does he admit he doesn't shower because it's too much trouble?

You may not be able to stay in a skilled nursing facility, but the best of these offer rooms to visiting family members, so ask or find accommodations nearby. Pop in at random times during the day and night while you are in town for a more complete picture of what's really going on.

Regardless of where your parent is living, the visit will be a good one for both of you if you plan ahead and stay long enough to provide comforting companionship as well as practical help. You don't want to be the adult child whose visit your parents dread because they know it means two exhausting days of nonstop appointments and ceaseless interrogation about every detail of their lives. Blend in and observe.

If you have siblings, these trips also provide an excellent time for you to share information with them and reevaluate your parent's care together—and reevaluation should occur every few months. As I mentioned before, it's important for the out-of-town adult child to avoid swooping in with a long list of changes to make and advice to deliver. Have compassion for those in the trenches, and let your appreciation for all they do pour over them. Listen carefully to their perspectives, for while you may notice things about your parent that they haven't, you're also in danger of overreacting to what you observe for the first time. So respect their opinions and they will be more likely to respect yours.

The biggest challenge for long-distance caregivers is knowing when to visit an aging parent and how long to stay, especially as the unpredictable end draws near. After around ten days of keeping vigil with my mom, I yearned to return to the comfort of my home, my husband, my cats, and the hummingbirds at my feeder. A bit in denial, I tried to convince myself that Mom could linger for weeks. That I should go home, and come back later. Yet I stayed until she died, and I'm so glad I did.

Due to her husband's disability, my friend Dana had a different experience that many people face for various reasons: she was unable to fly out to be with her failing mother. "Though I could only hear her voice, over time I could actually sense her drifting away from me. I had the mental image of her on a rustic piece of driftwood, floating out to sea, the current taking her out of my grasp. I was left on the lonely shore, waving my arms, totally helpless as the most significant person in my life was fading from my view." Heartbreaking, but anyone who has been the far-away child can relate.

Watching for Abuse

It pains me to have to include this section, but include it I must. Cruel, sick, abusive personalities prey on the most vulnerable. In our culture, the most vulnerable are the very young and the very old. Especially if you are the sole caregiver and you live out of town, be alert to abuse in any form. Don't tell yourself, "It must be my imagination," when you suspect an abusive situation just because you don't want to face it or don't have time to investigate it. In this, more than any other area of your parent's care, it's important to trust your intuition. Better to sound an alarm that later proves false than to stay silent while a horrible situation becomes even worse.

Financial abuse isn't the most crushing type of abuse, but it can still be devastating. News accounts abound of the latest financial scams perpetrated on elders. A common one is a phone call from someone pretending to be a grandchild. The "grandchild" claims to be stranded or under arrest in a foreign country and needs money for a plane ticket home or to pay bail. Grandparents who quickly hang up on all kinds of calls telling them they've won the lottery or a free vacation will fall victim to a plea from a grandchild—even if the caller doesn't sound like Jason or Kristin. (The scammers do their homework on the victim's family, so they will use the correct name.)

Sharon, seventy-six and recovering from recent surgery, immediately headed to a local MoneyGram office after a caller who identified himself as her grandson David said he'd been arrested in Mexico and needed $2,400. Employees at MoneyGram warned her about the notorious grandparent scam, but Sharon sent the money anyway.

"I never fell for a scam before," she said. "But this was love. I would do anything for my grandchild." Sadly, "anything" included similar responses to five more calls before the real David returned her frantic messages. The Florida widow had drained her nest egg and borrowed against her home to wire more than $15,000.[2]

In one year, more than 25,500 older Americans reported sending $110 million to scammers posing as family members and claiming an injury or arrest in a foreign country. "That's just the tip of the iceberg," says Steve Baker of the Federal Trade Commission. "At most, only about eight percent of victims ever report the crime."[3]

And it's not the only scam out there. As our aging population has grown, so too have incidents of elder exploitation. Elderly people are increasingly falling victim to bogus lottery and sweepstakes schemes, telemarketing scams, unscrupulous lending practices, investment fraud, and identity theft. Sadly, the most common form of exploitation is relatives bilking money from an aging loved one. It's estimated that, in all, older Americans are being swindled out of at least $2.9 billion a year.[4] Money most of them cannot afford to lose.

While love may be one lure extortionists use, loneliness is another. Stories abound of older seniors who casually mention, "I met this nice young man at the store, and he offered to come home with me and bring in my groceries." You'll want to follow up with your elder about this nice young man, because he may soon bilk her out of money to buy a car so he can get to work, or to pay medical bills for a baby that never seems to materialize. The ploys are plentiful.

My mother, an intelligent, savvy woman, fell victim to a telephone scam. She was in the middle of an interesting afternoon talk show when the phone rang and a friendly voice identified himself as an employee of her bank. He needed to confirm her account number, her debit card number, and her password. Without thinking, Mom pulled all that information out of her wallet and gave it to the caller. As soon as she hung up, she realized she had been scammed. She called my sister, who spent the rest of her day calling Mom's bank, canceling her debit card, and so on.

On one of my visits, Mom asked me to help her go through her check register to identify donations she could claim on her income tax return. After just a few pages, I realized she had written a preponderance of ten-dollar and fifteen-dollar checks to nonprofit organizations, some repeatedly. She told me it was because of the free stationery items they sent her. My good-hearted mom was treating each of those mailings as a bill to be paid—thus insuring that she received many subsequent mailings.

Where were all those items, I asked. Over in her credenza. I opened the credenza door, and out poured a veritable flood of day planners, calendars, address labels, and note pads. I helped Mom select the ones she really wanted and needed, and we tossed or donated the rest. She didn't have to "pay" those bills, I assured her—not even if they included a stamp or a nickel with the mailing. It wasn't the worst scam to which she could have fallen victim, but it was still eating away at her disposable income.

To monitor more serious scams, watch for unexplained credit card activity, account withdrawals that trigger penalties, recent unauthorized changes in the titling of financial documents, or an older adult's unease about someone's seeking control of assets.

Eldercare Locator, with the help of the National Center on Elder Abuse, has put together a free consumer guide, "Protect Your

Pocketbook: Tips to Avoid Financial Exploitation," available at www
.eldercare.gov (under "Tools and Resources," click on "Brochures").
Review material like this brochure when you visit your aging parent,
and then leave it behind for your loved one to peruse on his or her
own. Increase elders' awareness by sharing stories about others being
taken in by scams that you either hear about or read of in the newspaper. And for goodness sake, remind them that you and your siblings
will always let them know if one of their grandchildren is leaving the
country!

Most heartbreaking of all is physical abuse of elders. We've all
heard the horror stories of old-style nursing homes where patients are
overmedicated, over-restrained, or left for days soaking in their own
urine. Harder to detect are cases of elders who may be dehydrated
or literally starving due to lack of assistance with drinking or eating.
Regulatory agencies have accomplished much to end such despicable
practices, but you must be alert to any form of abuse that may creep
in to your parent's care surreptitiously. Investigators aren't present
in every facility on every shift. If your parent is bedridden and no
longer communicative, pop-in visits and intuition become even more
valuable.

A call to a geriatric manager in the city where Henry's elderly aunt
lived was the stimulus that got her out of an abusive situation. "We're
really troubled by what we saw," Henry told the manager. "Aunt Mae
didn't seem at all alert. She's always been a feisty woman, yet she
appeared to be quite fearful. We also noticed some bruises on her
arms and face, which her housekeeper ascribed to frequent falls. The
bottom line is, we're not so sure that's the reason.

"We couldn't stay around to check out our suspicions," Henry continued, "but we need to have *someone* step in and let us know what's
going on." The geriatric care manager referred Henry and his wife to a
geriatric social worker, who paid several visits to Aunt Mae and soon
determined that the older woman was a victim of abuse by her housekeeper. The social worker quickly took over, fired the housekeeper,

and got Aunt Mae a trusted attendant until he could find the needed residential placement for her.[5]

Old people do fall, it's true. And skin tends to thin as we age, making it more susceptible to bruising, especially if the older person is on a prescribed blood thinner. Still, it was more than the bruising that led Henry to make that critical call. He and his wife trusted their intuition, their sense that something wasn't right.

As terrible as financial and physical abuse can be, they are both easier to detect than emotional abuse. It's tough to prove that an aide told your aging mother, "If you complain about me again, you'll be sorry," even if she musters the courage to tell you. How do you measure the pain of cutting, sarcastic remarks leveled at your mom by health care workers, or insults directed at her inability to remain continent?

Dementia can be cruel not only to its victims but also to those in the vicinity of the person with dementia. The family of one assisted living resident had to insist on a change of room assignment for their sweet mom after they determined that her demented roommate was cussing at her, making fun of her, degrading her religious beliefs, and otherwise verbally abusing her day after day. No one deserves to live out their last days with such toxic abuse.

As the long-distance caregiver, during your visits, you must be extra-attentive to any of these indications that your parent is being abused. Also, consider staying long enough to form solid connections with home health care workers or aides in the facility where your parent lives. Not only will they be likely to treat your parent more kindly and patiently, but you'll also have someone to call during a crisis—or anytime you suspect you aren't getting the whole story. Having an "inside man" is important for monitoring your parent's care, especially from a distance. When necessary, get the proper authorities involved.

This next question must be asked: What if you, the adult-child caregiver, are the one being abused? Dementia and overall crankiness brought on by an accrual of losses in elders can lead them to say some pretty mean things. What if, after your roller bag is carefully stowed in the overhead compartment, you gaze out the window at the clouds from thirty thousand feet so your seatmate won't notice the tears in your eyes? Rather than reflecting on warm memories of your visit, you wonder why your parent was so angry, unappreciative, and just downright cruel. Comments like, "You're never here long enough to help. I don't know why you bother," or, "You never could do anything right. I don't know why you think I need you now," can sting long after they are delivered.

Hopefully it's a long plane ride, because you'll need that time to process all that happened and put it in proper perspective. Pray. Ask the Lord to show you if you disrespected your parent in any way, and if so, confess your sins. More likely, you will receive His peace along with the realization that you did all you could out of love, and it's OK for your efforts to go unrewarded here on earth. Your faithfulness pleases God.

Although it may not help much with demented parents, one expert on aging says the trip home may be less painful if you take the time to have a "good good-bye" at the end of your visit. "It's important that we touch, say words of love, talk about the next time together, give one last small gift of a joke, kind words, or smiles," writes Mary Pipher. "I encourage families to take plenty of time with good-byes. The good-bye is what lingers for good or ill. A well-done good-bye can salvage a difficult visit. A well-done good-bye can warm the cockles of the heart until the next visit."[6] And there will always be a next visit until the final good-bye.

Chapter 13

LEAVING A LEGACY

Even when I am old and gray, do not forsake me, O God, till
I declare your power to the next generation, your might to all
who are to come.

—Psalm 71:18

After my friend Jan's grandmother had passed away and the family was sorting through her belongings, they came across a small cardboard box carefully tied with string. Written on the box lid in her grandmother's shaky handwriting was the label, "String too short to use."

Certainly this find wasn't one of the family treasures in the material sense of the word. Why would anyone collect useless items? What granddaughter would run delighted through the house yelling, "Look! Grandma left me some string too short to use!" Yet it was a legacy of sorts.

That she took the time to save all those tiny bits of string over the years tells the family something about their grandma. Having lived through the Great Depression, she was frugal. She didn't want to throw away anything someone else might use someday. She was thoughtful—and optimistic. Maybe someone would discover a way to cleverly reconnect bits of string, and if so, her family would be ready! Or perhaps she envisioned a beautiful cut-string decoupage. That small, labeled box was a part of her legacy.

So often in the writing of this book, I've wanted to pick up the phone and ask my mom for some point of clarity. *What were the words to that song you were humming right after you moved into assisted living? What was my friend's mother's first name? How did you keep your sense of humor through it all? Were you scared when you signed those hospice papers?*

Going through old albums, I've wanted to ask her about the people in the photos. Not just their names or familial relationship but who they were to her. Did she like them? Did they like her? How did she know?

Beyond dishes, jewelry, and furniture, my mother left me a rich heritage of memories, family stories, faith, and love. In addition, our whole family often quotes what I coined as "momilies" from my mom—like homilies but less preachy. We say, "Katie, bar the door" in times of trouble and "I'll swan" when something truly amazing happens. On a really busy day, there are "no flies on us," and when something is perfectly ready it is "all saucered and blowed" (as you do with hot coffee before you drink it). Strange as it is to hear the same momilies my mom used coming out of my own mouth, I'm glad I'm passing them on. After all, she wasn't "just whistling Dixie." Yet it's never enough, is it? Once our parents are gone, we are left wanting more. More momilies, more laughs, more time.

There is a wonderful, bathed-in-light, blessed window of time that I pray you will be given with your aging parent. Once the hard decisions are made, the family home is cleared out and sold, the medical protocol is in place, and the new living arrangements are mostly working, there can come a period of relief: a time of recuperation from all the struggles you and your parent have both experienced.

If you are given the opportunity to have this time together, be it a few weeks or many years, embrace it and savor it. Congratulate yourselves on making it to this point. Take a deep breath. Fall into an easy routine of visits and phone calls, meals and memories. But also use this season before everything changes again, next time even more dramatically, to encourage your aging parent to reflect back over a life well-lived and be intentional about the legacy he or she wants to leave you and those who follow you. To do so is to give a gift beyond compare. You will be helping your mom or dad finish well—in a way that honors the Creator of life. And it will make the letting go that follows so much easier for both of you.

Each of us will leave a legacy. The only question is, what kind of legacy will it be? Will our descendants be repulsed or apathetic when they hear our names in years to come, or will they be warmed by the memories our names evoke? We honor our elders when we talk to them about their legacies and encourage them that it's not too late to leave the kind of legacy they desire.

As I interviewed caregivers about their lingering memories of their departed parents, and what they missed most about them, the descriptions were poignant. Pam said, "As I think of Flora, it is with such fondness and laughter at things we enjoyed before the process of 'going out' began. I really think that is her gift to me, that she was always such a positive, independent, and interested person; that she left me with her presence, and it is lovely." Don remembers that "my mom was a wonderful cook. Homemade yeast rolls, apricot fried pies, 'Company's Coming' pie. I miss how I would just hug her and not let go when we were both older. Since I was so much taller, I remember the light scent of her hairspray. Before my dad died, he would ride with me up into the Arkansas mountains to go antiquing. I have warm, personal memories of those afternoons with him."

Even the little things evoked by memories of laughter, flavors, and fragrances become a part of our legacy.

So how do we assist our elders in passing on their legacies? Obviously the lives they've lived are faits accomplis. We can't help them re-create professional careers, the birthing and rearing of children, vacations taken, and friendships made. But we *can* help them realize that all these facets of their long lives are integral to the proud legacy they leave behind.

One woman who volunteers with elders likes to say, when someone dies, that they have "graduated." As we have the chance to prepare our parents for graduation day, we want to help them into a graduation gown stitched with memories to cherish, and we want to place a mortarboard on their heads that will suffice as an earthly crown until they receive their heavenly ones. We want them to leave this world feeling not old and used up but exclaiming, "Wow! That was quite a ride!" Your encouragement that they be intentional about their legacies can go a long way toward giving your elders this kind of sendoff, regardless of how they have lived to date or how grumpy they may be about growing old.

You've probably heard the admonition that in graveyards all over the world are tombstones engraved with two dates: the date of birth and the date of death. Between these two dates is a dash. The dash symbolizes the life we live. The question is, how will we spend the dash?

For some time now, you have been trying to stretch and enhance your elderly parent's dash. Now help your mom or dad to look kindly at the life behind, tie up loose ends, and look forward with hope to the eternal life to come. Help your seniors define their legacies and take pride in them. You've probably already helped with sorting furniture, clothes, knickknacks, and photo albums. You may have also helped with the drawing up of a will to direct the disbursement of accumulated wealth, stocks and bonds, and other material possessions. Good for you. There's peace of mind that comes with getting all that done, for you and your family as well as for your parent. But that's not the kind of legacy we are discussing here, because it's not the legacy that matters most.

Herbert Brokering, eighty, decided to record the legacy he wanted to leave for his family and others in a book titled *I Will to You: Leaving a Legacy for Those You Love*. In the introduction he writes, "Not everything of value is covered in a legal document. A legal will is made to take care of big things, concrete matters, property, investments. My children know where my will is. That is not all I have to give. Much of what we cherish most is gathered in small pieces through the years. What about this view of an oak tree outside my window, a song that makes me smile, this dried rose and its memories, last night's compassionate dream? What about the apology I want to offer . . . the hopes I cherish?"[1]

As a result, the author came up with one hundred things he wanted to pass along to others as part of his legacy and collected them in his book. What does he will? The essays expound on favorite things, places to be, sights to see, and a world to come. "One hundred is not many," he writes. "Some of you will have many more bequests of your own. . . . If my thoughts stir your own ideas, your own songs, your own legacy, I am thankful. Then I am at peace! End-of-life matters really matter all of life. Keeping the end in mind helps us to make the journey."[2]

One word of caution: the process of establishing a legacy should be a gentle one. The last thing our elders want is to be badgered with a lot of questions each time we visit. They also don't need a long to-do list at this stage of life. On one of the last days I visited my friend Myrtle in hospice before she passed away, she whispered to me, "I feel like I'm leaving behind a suitcase full of old tissues." I took that to mean she felt she had left some things undone. I comforted her as best I could, reminding her of many of the things she had accomplished in her lifetime: books published, children changed, people loved. All of us will no doubt leave this life thinking we could have done more, yet the Lord assures us that everything will be complete in the end.

Read through the following ways a legacy can be reinforced and see which, if any, you can still approach with your loved one, ever so gently and without badgering. Working on legacy-building together can be bonding and give your aging parent a sense of restored purpose. But don't push it. Let it evolve naturally, perhaps limiting yourself to only one question or legacy discussion each time you visit.

The Legacy of Family History

Every family should be gifted with a genealogist to record all the branches and fruits of family trees, but we aren't all so blessed. Fortunately, computer searches like Ancestry.com can fill in the gaps if you are inclined to become an amateur genealogist yourself. This can be a fun activity for you and your elderly adult to explore side by side in front of a computer. Perhaps curiosity will even spur his or her development of more advanced computer skills.

More important than knowing your family is descended from barons or pirates, however, is learning what your parents know about more recent ancestors before they pass away and their knowledge is lost. None of us wants to be asked by a child, "How are we related to Uncle Fred?" only to realize we have no idea because we didn't listen when our mother explained it for the umpteenth time.

Your mom or dad may enjoy sitting next to you on the couch on a quiet winter's afternoon looking through old photo albums. This time, pay attention to who's who. Identify people and capture stories with captions or sticky notes. You'll be helping to preserve the family legacy for your own children and grandchildren.

Amazingly, long-term memory may become sharper with age, and oral histories are wonderful, a gift for the ages. Families have had success in recording oral histories themselves by sitting down with a tape recorder or video camera. Others use services like StoryCorps to do the job for them. The key is to elicit open, free-flowing memories from your older adults, not scripted answers to questions. If you are doing the recording, sometimes it's best if you don't tell your elderly person that you are recording until afterwards, but that's for you to decide.

The day when I decided to video some of my mother's memories, she was still living in her home in Tennessee. After two days of saying, "Oh, I couldn't possibly do that. What do I have to say, anyway?" she finally agreed to sit for our taping. She showed up at the appointed time, all spiffed up, and sat down in the kitchen chair with the posture and attitude of a celebrity. As soon as the camera was recording, she adopted her most charming storytelling voice, and I got some wonderful stories about her life as a little girl, how she met my dad, where they lived when they were first married, and more.

I was so excited, though, that I forgot to stop and check the video quality. The lighting isn't great, though capturing something is better than nothing. From my experience, though, I would say it might be wise to use the professionals. I thought Mom would be more relaxed with me, but those who specialize in recording the life stories of seniors usually know how to put their subjects at ease.

Books can also be purchased that create an instant memoir by asking questions and providing space for answers. I suspect far more of these have been given as gifts than have actually been filled out, but it's another option to consider. As a compromise, you could buy one of these books, take it with you on visits, and then ask the questions and jot down your parent's answers. Again, recording is easier, but seniors may enjoy knowing they are essentially writing a memoir.

Whichever format you choose, here are some possible warm-up questions to get you started with your own interview:

- Where and when were you born?
- What do you remember of your mother and father?
- How did you spend your free time as a child?
- What friends or activities do you remember?
- Where did you go to elementary and high school?
- Did you go to college? Where? What are your best memories of those years?
- Did you take family vacations? Where did you love to go?

Let your subject get comfortable with the format first. You can delve into more difficult, personal subjects such as relationships, religion, and regrets at another time. Begin by giving elders permission to "pass" on anything they don't want to discuss. You'll sense when enough is enough.

Lastly, ask them how they would most like to be remembered—and make a note of the answer.

The Legacy of Forgiveness

I'm constantly amazed how many issues come to light in our assisted living Bible study when we cover a lesson on forgiveness. People in their eighties and nineties can still harbor a decades-old grudge against a father who deserted the family, a sister who never writes, or a first husband who was a cad. The inability to forgive can not only depress the unforgiving person, but it can make him or her physically ill—especially when the grudge has festered for a lifetime. It is said that not forgiving someone is like drinking poison and waiting for the other person to die.

But the good news is that through the power of the Holy Spirit, we can forgive those who refuse to forgive us, those who refuse to say they are sorry, even those who have already passed away. So as painful as it may be, explore with your aging parent any areas where forgiveness is needed in order for them to leave this world unshackled by anger and resentment. If a phone call needs to be made or a note written, gently nudge your loved one to take that step. Help if necessary.

Remember to also pray together for forgiveness for the two of you—for those shortcomings and sins you are aware of and any that have conveniently escaped your attention. However, if you have had a contentious relationship with your parent all your life, this is probably not the time to go into the specifics of every offense. Just as holiday gatherings aren't the place to bring up lifelong grievances with parents or siblings, neither is the winter of your parents' lives.

If you still seek your parents' blessing for your own well-being, it's

OK to ask for it. Just be prepared for rejection—and forgive them for their inability to provide what you seek. It may be more productive to say something like, "I know we haven't always been all we could have been to one another, but I want you to know I forgive you for that, and I hope you can forgive me." Blanket forgiveness is better than no forgiveness at all. Seal it with a hug.

Forgiveness is a legacy issue, because resentments and anger can affect future generations. If a brother and sister have a falling out over a family inheritance, for example, and decide as adults to speak to one another as little as possible, then their children may be denied the gift of having close cousins in their lives. We want to encourage our elders to work out their differences with family members if possible, not pass them down to the next generation.

I love this quote from the theologian Henri Nouwen: "Forgiveness means that I continually am willing to forgive the other person for not being God—for not fulfilling all my needs. I, too, must ask forgiveness for not being able to fulfill other people's needs. . . . The interesting thing is that when you can forgive people for not being God, then you can celebrate that they are a reflection of God."[3] None of us is God, but we can all reflect Him when we are able to forgive as He forgave us, giving His Son to die for our sins.

Older people who harbor grudges for many years often say, "I'll forgive, but I'll never forget." Pastor Chuck Swindoll believes that for believers, canceling the debt is how you create a legacy of forgiveness. "Whether our dispute is a personal or a public matter, we quickly reveal whether we possess a servant's heart in how we respond to those who have offended us. We always have a choice. Will we choose to hold on to the things that have hurt us until we've erected monuments of spite that divide our once harmonious relationships . . . or will we choose to create lasting legacies of forgiveness by forgiving those that hurt us and then releasing the offense?"[4] Encourage seniors you love to choose forgiveness, and in so doing to cancel any debt that not forgiving would carry forward to the next generation.

The Legacy of Grandparenting

Every Wednesday, my sister Mary babysat her first granddaughter, Avery. She always took Avery with her to check on my mother in assisted living, and I'm not sure who loved it most. Avery, three, would run down the hall toward Nana's room as fast as her little feet could take her. My mom kept a stuffed cat as a "pet," and Avery always wanted to pat the kitty. She also got a piece of candy out of the candy jar on Nana's coffee table. And she got lots of hugs and smiles from my mom. No wonder she loved it.

The other residents began to look forward to Avery's visits too, and would save up things to give her. My mom enjoyed being able to show off her precious great-granddaughter, so she didn't mind sharing. Whenever I called my mom, she would regale me with the latest story about something cute Avery did or said. I silently wished she could know my own geographically distant grandchildren in the same way, since I thought they were pretty darn cute too, but I understood. Avery was the one Mom got to see the most. And she came along at a time in my mother's life when there were few distractions from focusing on this one precious great-grandchild. It was a match made in heaven, and my sister was so thoughtful to make it happen for both of them.

Reams have been written on the grandparenting experience, and we can't begin to explore all the benefits and blessings of the connection between grandparents and their grandchildren and great-grandchildren here. We should, however, consider a few points when it comes to legacy building.

Your role as the intermediary between the generations is to maximize their exposure to one another. Make sure your aging parent has lots of birthday cards on hand to send to grandchildren far away. Mark the dates on an easy-to-read calendar and provide the stamps. Arrange as many visits as possible. Share stories about each generation with the other. In other words, do what you can to build the bridge.

In his wonderful book *Aging: The Fulfillment of Life*, Henri Nouwen wrote, "Our first and most important task is to help the elderly become our teachers again and to restore the broken connections between the generations."[5] Take your responsibility to do this seriously. The rewards will be great.

Marty Norman wrote a poignant book, *Generation G*, about her experiences being a twenty-first-century grandmother. I love that she describes us as rich, savvy, and silver: rich in experiences, savvy about life, and silver instead of gray. Her short essays explore all aspects of being a grandmother, and in the one titled "Going Out in Style" she says, "At my last breath, I hope they think I breathed life upon their world, that in everything I touched, in everything I did, I brought life and healing rather than death and despair. I hope that my presence planted a garden in their lives."[6] Me too, Marty, me too. Inasmuch as that is the kind of grandparent we want to be, we should encourage our aging parents to seriously tend to their own grandparenting legacy.

The Legacy of Faith

Even young people think about dying and are curious about heaven. The presence of elders keeps us all mindful that we too are aging. All our lives we are preparing, in a way, for the day when we come into our rightful position as the oldest generation. If your mom's faith is strong and she has the blessed assurance of knowing that she will be with the Lord in heaven when she dies, encourage her to share her excitement with her children and grandchildren. Not only will she be giving them a powerful witness of faith but she will be preparing them for losing her someday. Their grief will be much easier to bear when they know she is where she always said she would be—celebrating on the streets of heaven.

And once she shares her confidence about where she is going, it will be more natural for her to share the truth of God's plan of salvation with her grandchildren—to tell them that Jesus died for their sins so they can go to heaven too and see her again someday. Leading our children and grandchildren closer to the Lord is the most important legacy we can leave.

Before a visit with grandkids, encourage your elders to pray for the guidance and words of wisdom they want to share. Suggest that they ask the Lord to bring to mind meaningful stories from the many in the anthology of their minds. If they are willing to prepare through prayer, the Lord will honor their intent.

Are we ever too old to tell stories? Quite the contrary: the longer we live, the more stories we have to tell. Passing along the stories of our lives is a way to leave a legacy for our children and grandchildren. How else will they know what it was like when we were growing up, or how our country survived depression and war, if we don't tell them the stories? Hearing about relatives both deceased and living helps children understand their place in the world. The stories give them roots and can even provide the confidence and inspiration they need to succeed.

Of course, no story we tell will ever have as much impact as the story of how we came into a relationship with the Lord. Sharing our stories is the easiest way to share our faith, because our relationship with the Lord is ours and ours alone. No one can tell our story except us, and no one can ever say it isn't true when we have experienced it firsthand. In 1 Peter 3:15 we read, "Always be prepared to give an answer to everyone who asks you to give the reason for the hope that you have. But do this with gentleness and respect." Never is that more important than in elders' conversations with the children and grand-children who love them.

We know what the Lord has done in our lives. No matter what else we have forgotten, we remember those times when He intervened to bless us or send us in a different direction. The details are likely crystal clear, but if not, we can ask Him to remind us and He will. A story that gives someone the hope of glory is a story that must be told. Encourage your older loved ones to tell theirs.

And remind them that being prayer warriors is also a part of their legacy. Even the frailest elders can pray for children and grandchildren, and those heartfelt prayers have great purpose and power in the kingdom of God. As long as we are still breathing, we have purpose in this life and a mission to fulfill. Prayer is a powerful part of our purpose and mission. When interviewed late in life, Billy Graham said, "I've learned that even if we can't do everything we once did, God isn't finished with us, and we can still serve Him."[7]

Sadly, not all of our seniors have a testimony of faith to share. If your parent has rejected God earlier in life or has spent a lifetime sitting on the fence without coming down on the side of surrender to the Lord, then leaving a spiritual legacy may not be possible. Yet it's never too late for you to share your faith, your story, one more time, and to pray for a late-in-life salvation experience for your parent.

Even if you aren't given assurance that your parent will be with the Lord when he or she dies, rest in the knowledge that it is God who decides who enters into eternal life. He is God and we aren't. When it comes to having to say good-bye to a parent who refuses to believe, there is comfort in that truth. Pray, let go of your loved one, and trust God. We never know what miracles He may choose to work in the lives of those we love—right up until their last breath.

Chapter 14

LETTING GO

*The LORD will keep you from all harm—he will watch over
your life; the LORD will watch over your coming and going
both now and forevermore.*

—Psalm 121:7–8

I was blessed to be with my mother for two weeks before she passed
away at ninety-two. Sitting beside her bed, I found myself drawn
to her hands—wanting to touch them and hold them as long as I
possibly could. These were the hands that cared for me when I was
little and reached out for me when we crossed the street—both when
I was small and carefree and when she was old and frail. These were
the hands that created the home my two sisters and I remember so
fondly—the hands that stirred the gravy, tied the bows on the backs
of our dresses, decorated the Christmas tree, and folded the laundry.

On family vacations my mom would lay her arm across the back
of the front seat where she sat with my dad, tapping her fingers in

time to the music on the car radio or to the songs she was teaching us. I remember marveling at her long red nails and sparkly rings and thinking my mom's hands had to be the most beautiful hands in the world!

As she aged, arthritis took its toll on those hands, but they were still beautiful to me because they were the hands that clapped excitedly whenever Mom first saw me on my visits to Tennessee from Colorado. And when she wanted to call her three daughters together one last time and it was so difficult for her to speak, she motioned to us with her hands. Saying, "I want one, two, three," as she pointed to three spots on the foot of her bed, she indicated that she expected us all to be present at once. When we were assembled, in an incredible and memorable blessing, she told us how much she loved us, how proud she was of us, and thanked us for taking good care of her in her old age. Then she sang the words "He touched me" from the old hymn, and simply said the word, "Peace."

Mom lingered for two more days but never really spoke or opened her eyes again. She had said her good-byes. As I sat by her bed after she had slipped away, I was still holding her hand and wondering how I could ever let it go. How I could ever let *her* go. But I had no choice.

The letting-go process—and it is a process composed of events and emotions over time—is so much easier to bear when the person who is dying has participated in the decisions leading up to final departure. When they have signed the hospice papers instructing everyone involved to put all their energies into providing care but not cure. When they have said good-bye and "I love you." Even when it's a prolonged good-bye, just having a good-bye makes letting go so much easier emotionally.

In contrast, when someone we love dies suddenly, as my father did at age sixty-eight of a heart condition in his sleep, there follows an emotional grasping to hold on, a sense of disbelief and shock. Yet again, we have no choice but to let go. The sooner we are able to do so, the sooner we can continue to live the lives we ourselves have been given to live. Hopefully, because of our letting-go experiences, our lives are richer in meaning, gratitude, and love than they were before. We honor those we have lost when we go on living joyfully, in gratitude for the lives they lived—thus keeping the best of what they left to us alive.

Letting go can actually be a relief for a weary caregiver. Jeanine had spent weeks trying to coax her dad into drinking and eating to keep up his strength during the last weeks of his life. "I finally made the decision to stop wasting what little time we had left together, and I tried to replace the harshness and scolding with acceptance, unconditional love, and lots of affirmation," she said. "He needed that. Turns out, so did I."

Too Soon to Let Go

In chapter 8, "Living with the Aging Body," we talked about advance medical directives that can be of huge assistance to caregivers helping someone chart out a journey toward the end of life. We discussed those matters in that chapter rather than this one because once the letting go process is underway, it may be too late for the dying person to participate in making those key decisions. Especially in cases of dementia, including Alzheimer's, what a gift it is to the family for the patient to make his or her wishes known while still possessed of a sound mind. Putting such instructions in place is a greater gift for sons and daughters than a safe full of gold.

I've been a fan of Ellen Goodman's writing for decades. Her life seemed to parallel mine in significant ways as she wrote about parenting, friendship, and midlife challenges. So I wasn't surprised to discover that she has weighed in on the subject of caring for older parents and on the importance of talking about their end-of-life wishes with some specificity.

"My mom and I talked about everything, but we'd never had a conversation about what she wanted at the end of life that went any deeper than, 'If I'm ever like that, pull the plug,' Goodman told Paula

Span of the *New York Times*. "Then there was a long decline," Ms. Goodman said ruefully, "and no plug to pull."[1]

As a result of her experience, Goodman compassionately set about to make sure others didn't find themselves in the same predicament she found herself in with her ninety-two-year-old mom. She founded The Conversation Project (www.theconversationproject.org), a website that aims to encourage end-of-life discussions. The starter kit on the site offers reassuring hand-holding as well as concrete topics to tackle, and it helps measure the intensity of people's feelings.

"I do think we've hit a tipping point," Goodman continued in the interview, pointing out that we Baby Boomers who are now watching our parents age have been forces for change all of our lives. "This is a subject we've been slow to grapple with," she said. "And I think people really are ready."[2]

Yet just because directives are in place and conversations have been held and documented, there is no reason for our elders to just sit and wait to die. There's often a lot of life to live even after a terminal diagnosis. Knowing the end of a novel because we saw the movie doesn't take away the joy of reading the engaging prose or following the intricate plotlines. Living each and every day we are given is a gift we need to help our elders embrace. Colors seem more vivid, hugs linger longer, stars shine brighter when experienced by someone who is grateful for one more day. As the old adage says, it's not the number of breaths we take that matter most; it's the moments that take our breath away. Those in the process of dying are best qualified to embrace that truth.

A dear older woman I know, in her midnineties, signed up for hospice care after receiving several dire diagnoses simultaneously. Her family rallied around, her adult children worked through all the options for her care, but then, to everyone's surprise, the woman began to feel better. So well, in fact, that she decided to put hospice care on hold, move into an assisted living apartment, and fully enjoy whatever time she had left.

One organization in Arizona, the Bucket List Foundation (www

.bucketlistfoundation.org), believes so strongly in helping seniors get the most out of the latter part of their lives that they raise money to fund last wishes. Founded by hospice nurse Kimberly Iverson, the foundation sends seniors to ballgames, reunites family members, plans dream vacations—whatever the terminal patient says he or she wants to experience before dying. "Living each day to the fullest because tomorrow isn't promised" is the organization's motto.

My dear friend Alice helped her husband, Jim, make the most of his last six months. When Jim learned he had melanoma and it had metastasized, he opted not to undergo chemotherapy or other treatments. Instead, he and Alice went on a trip to see old friends, and his two brothers came to visit from Scotland. I went to visit about ten days before Jim died. He was propped up on the couch, their beloved little dog curled up next to him, watching an armament-intensive movie with his son and son-in-law for some heavy-duty male bonding.

Jim, only seventy-four, knew it wasn't the number of years in his life that mattered but the life in his years. He didn't let go until it was time. He also blessed his wife of over fifty years by telling her, "After I'm gone, don't ever think about what you might have done differently. You've taken wonderful care of me. We've said everything that needs to be said and done everything that needs to be done. I'm ready to go." Their parting was still agonizing and grief-filled for Alice, of course, but not letting go too soon was a wonderful gift for both of them.

Other gifts those with terminal diagnoses can give their families are the tying up of loose ends, the passing on of blessings of all kinds, and the blessed assurance that they know where they are going when they die. We are all dying. The dying process begins the day we are born. But those with reason to believe they are going to die sooner rather than later have a powerful witness to share when they face death believing in eternal life through faith in Jesus Christ.

While it may be too soon to let go, it's never too soon for those with terminal diagnoses to sign up for hospice care. Hospice is a unique blend of services that address the physical, emotional, and spiritual needs of the terminally ill and their families. Hospice can help the patient and the family make all the difficult decisions to come and can manage pain and all the other symptoms that arise.

I once interviewed a woman whose husband had recently signed up for hospice care. She said, "It feels like we've just landed on big, soft pillows." My friend Alice said she felt surrounded by angels after meeting the hospice workers assigned to Jim and her during his illness.

People sometimes have the misconception that you don't need hospice care until death is imminent, but that's simply not true. Focusing on comfort and pain management rather than cure, hospice services can make the whole dying process much more bearable for everyone. If someone you love has a terminal diagnosis and has decided to forego additional medical intervention and treatment, it may be too soon to let go, but it's not too soon for hospice care.

Too Hard to Let Go

There's no end to the list of procedures that can be employed to prevent a body from dying. Medical considerations, moral and religious considerations, ethical considerations, and legal considerations can all come into play. In the absence of advance directives from their loved ones, families are left to sort out all the options themselves, with the help of the medical community, and their individual beliefs and preferences can often conflict.

Hank Dunn served as a hospice chaplain and so was often privy to the agonizing discussions families have as a loved one nears death. In his book, *Hard Choices for Loving People*, he recounts some of these encounters. Often he has been able to help a family member make a decision merely by asking a well-timed question. When a friend came to him distraught about whether to continue her eighty-two-year-old mother's dialysis treatment, Dunn asked, "How effectively is the dialysis working?" The woman replied, "The doctors say it isn't doing any good." Dunn then asked the question that would lead to real revelation for his friend.

I asked, "Did your mother ever give any indication of what she would have wanted?"

"Yes. She said she never wanted to be on dialysis."

As the two friends continued their conversation, it was discovered that the daughter was attempting to prolong her mother's life to assuage her own guilt for not spending enough time with her mother in recent years.[3]

According to Dunn, it sometimes seems easier for medical professionals to aggressively treat patients for years than to confront the emotional and spiritual issues that drive the treatment choices. Doctors are trained to do everything medically possible to treat a patient's physical body, while little to no training is given in dealing with the caregiver's emotional and spiritual needs. The consequence? In these situations, doctors are often "treating the wrong patient."[4]

None of us wants to be that wrong patient. We don't want to put our beloved mom through painful tests or procedures that will do nothing to extend her life or improve its quality. Yet it happens— day after day in hospital after hospital. Often procedures are ordered without a family's knowledge. Other times, siblings disagree and are in different stages of the letting-go process. Because one wants to try the aggressive treatment, the others concede.

Medical professionals are not in the business of torturing old people. Doctors don't order tests and procedures to be cruel, but rather because they have been trained to intervene in every medical way possible and may not have been trained in the art of dying well. It takes a well-documented advance directive on file, or a family united emotionally and spiritually, to prevent such abuse of our elders. And abuse it can be.

Chaplains and others in ministry agree that it is often hardest for adult children to let go of their aging parents, and to forego useless treatments, if they haven't come to terms with their own mortality, and if they lack a strong belief in the life everlasting. An aging mom can help set the stage for her own more naturally occurring death by making her wishes known earlier in life and by assuring her children and grandchildren that she knows, without a doubt, that she will be dancing in the streets of heaven when she dies. Who among us, looking around a hospital room filled with IV bags, medications, and an oxygen tank or respirator, would want to keep our loved one there against her will?

Is there ever a reason to intervene to prevent or delay death? Certainly. CPR is appropriate for a seventy-year-old experiencing a heart attack but with a full prospect of recovery and perhaps twenty more years of life to enjoy. It's not as appropriate to administer it to a ninety-year-old in the hospital, who could be left breathing but with broken ribs because of the procedure.

Artificial hydration and nutrition (AHN) is often employed to make a dying person more comfortable, but the question needs to be asked: If this person has voluntarily stopped drinking and eating because his body is telling him it's time to close up shop, who are we to prevent that from happening? Occasionally an older person is left on life support or given AHN so a distant child can arrive at the bedside and squeeze a warm hand as she says good-bye. No one would argue with such a decision.

The end result is always the same, however. At some point, we all have to let go. "My message to those who are taking this journey to letting go is one of hope," Hank Dunn writes. "The Creator has granted life as a gift. For me to hold on and grasp out of fear is to deny the gift and the Giver. Having walked this journey to letting go with hundreds of patients and families, I only have a greater sense of the wonderfulness of life."[5]

Home Free

Much is being said and written in this century about the "good death" and how we all want to achieve it. What's interesting about this is, we are all saying we want the kind of death most people experienced before medical technology intervened. We envision a death where someone we love is dabbing our brow with a cool cloth. Family members are gathered around singing hymns and praying. We've lived a full life. We've said our good-byes, confessed our sins, asked for forgiveness if necessary, and we are ready to go home in the real sense—to be home free, running full speed into the arms of our Lord and Savior.

Katy Butler, author of the insightful and personal book about dying well titled *Knocking on Heaven's Door*, explains the situation statistically. "Three-quarters of Americans want to die at home, as their ancestors did," she writes, "but only a quarter of the elderly do. Two-fifths of deaths now take place in a hospital, an institution where only the destitute and the homeless died before the dawn of the twentieth century. Most of us say we don't want to die 'plugged into machines,' but a fifth of American deaths now take place in intensive care, where ten days of futile flailing can cost as much as $323,000."[6]

Katy watched her beautiful, talented, creative mother orchestrate her own "good death" shortly before her eighty-fifth birthday. Sometimes tortured by the longing to do something to save her mom, Katy nevertheless also felt proud of her mom for taking charge of her own destiny. For six years, she had cared for her husband, who had been given a pacemaker too hastily and thus torturously outlived his mind and natural body. Katy's mom didn't want that for herself. When the doctors suggested life-saving heart surgery and listed the possible outcomes, she respectfully declined. Instead, she slept in her own bed the night before she died and faced death graciously and courageously in the hospital the next day.

In a report to the *Wall Street Journal*, Butler wrote, "Why don't we die the deaths we want to die? In part because we say we want good deaths but act as if we won't die at all. In part because life-saving technologies have erased the once-bright line between saving a life and prolonging a dying. In part because saying, 'Just shoot me' is not a plan. Above all, we've forgotten what our ancestors knew: that preparing for a 'good death' is not a quickie process to save for the panicked ambulance ride to the emergency room. The decisions we make and refuse to make long before we die help determine our pathway to the final reckoning."[7]

As dire as the dying process can be, even in the best of circumstances, it may surprise you to know that there's plenty of room for humor. On any given day, a mixture of laughter and tears is almost guaranteed among those who keep bedside vigils. In the last days of my mom's life, she was in her pretty bed in her assisted living apartment, all propped up on pillows. To ease her breathing, she was given oxygen; she had a cannula connected to a large oxygen tank by a long rubber tube that extended down the side of the bed and across the floor. One by one, Mom's assisted living friends knocked softly on the door and came in to say good-bye to their friend. At one point I realized her dear friend Molly was standing on the oxygen hose, essentially cutting off Mom's oxygen. I didn't want to embarrass Molly, so I was able to gently guide her closer to Mom to say her tearful good-byes—and move the tube out from under her feet. The last thing Molly would have wanted was to hasten Mom's departure!

Carol Bradley Bursack tells a humorous story about her mother's roommate in a nursing home, an Alzheimer's patient named Mavis. During the three-day period prior to her mother's death, Carol and her sister kept vigil. "During this time," Carol writes, "the nursing home staff tried their best to divert Mavis and keep her from Mom's room during the day, but, alas, the room also belonged to Mavis. And Mavis was quick. She was also sneaky. So, on the first day of our death vigil, as Beth and I spoke soft words of good-bye to Mom, Mavis suddenly popped her head around the dividing curtain and hollered, 'Is she dead yet?' She then sighed, shook her little gray head, and quietly murmured, 'I loved her so.' Beth and I were startled to say the least."

Over the three days, Mavis kept checking in with the same question, "Is she dead yet?" and the same sweet sentiment, "I loved her so." After a while, Carol and her sister decided there was nothing to do but laugh. "The whole scene felt like a sitcom," she wrote.[8]

Humor in the midst of pain and loss is a beautiful thing. Don't feel guilty about laughing if something humorous happens. Just let it go. You will need the stress relief humor brings, and the healing too.

Every human being has the right to decide how he or she would prefer to die, given a choice. Yet I am not advocating physician-assisted suicide or euthanasia, because I believe each day we live is ordained by God. He may choose to extend a life beyond what we believe to be reasonable, but from His perspective, there is a reason for that person to still be alive.

I think back to those last days when my mother was unresponsive and seemed to us to be gone but was still alive. Why didn't the Lord go ahead and take her? Then I peeked into the bedroom while an aide was changing Mom's bed, rolling her small body side to side to replace the sheet below her. Tears were flowing unchecked down the young woman's face. What encounters with my mom was she remembering—conversations to which my sisters and I had not been privy? What work was the Lord doing in her heart that day to prepare her for her own death? For her own entrance to eternal life? God is God and we are not. He has His reasons.

It was another encounter between my mother and her hospice nurse that gave me peace and the certainty my mother was ready to go. I don't think Mom knew I was still in the room, as it would have been her nature to spare me such a painful conversation. She sat up in bed, grabbed Donna's arm as she was adjusting Mom's oxygen, looked Donna right in the eyes, and asked, "Will you let me die?" Donna assured her that while she would not help her die, yes, when the time came she would not intervene. She would let her die. Mom said, "Thank you," with all the Southern graciousness she could muster, laid back down, and closed her eyes. At almost ninety-three, my mother was surely aware of the agonizing, prolonged deaths of people she had known. She didn't want a death like that for herself. Praise God, she didn't have one; she passed away shortly thereafter on August 9, 2008. Epicurus wrote, "The art of living well and the art of dying well are one." We were blessed that my mom did both.

My mother-in-law's passing, almost eight months before my mom's, came as more of a shock, but it was peaceful all the same. On Christmas Day, 2007, my husband and I spent a good part of the afternoon in Mary Frances's room in the skilled nursing facility. We knew she was frail. Attempts to celebrate her ninety-second birthday with lunch and a cake in the facility's private dining room together four days earlier had been punctuated by her requests to "please just take me back to bed," but we had no idea death was so near. Jim read the Christmas story from Luke and other Scripture verses to comfort her, and we prayed for healing for her broken hip. From her bed, she commented occasionally, but mostly she slipped in and out of sleep.

When we rose to leave, I walked over to pull the covers up over Mary Frances's arms. As I leaned in close, she said, "Thank you, Nancy. You are always so considerate." As a caregiver, I knew I had tried. But I also thought I could have done so much more. Her generous words brought tears to my eyes.

Jim gave her a kiss on the forehead, we both told her we loved her, and then we left. How shocking it was to receive the call the very next day that she had died in her sleep. We were blessed that her parting was as peaceful as it was.

Losing both of our moms in a period of eight months took a toll on us emotionally. No wonder that in the fall of 2008, I anxiously awaited the first snow. There's an almost spiritual quality about the first snow. Softly and silently it covers the last of the rusty old leaves in the gutters and curbsides, the stained driveways, and the potholed roads. Similarly, it seems to cover all the pain and disappointment of the past year, sending the heavenly message, "See? All things can be clean and new again."

That year, my husband and I needed that comforting, healing first snow more than ever. Although our moms passed away in care facilities far apart, our recollections of days spent in assisted living centers, hospitals, and skilled nursing units were similar. We hadn't forgotten all the blessings that came our way—coming across caring doctors or nurses just when they were needed most; getting that open bed we were told wouldn't be available; arriving in time to say "good-bye" and "I love you." Nor did we question our mothers' joyful eternal lives near the heavenly "storehouses of the snow" (Job 38:22).

But as anyone who has been a caregiver to a dying loved one can understand, we also had haunting memories of conflicting medical advice, sleeplessness, and pain management.

Could the first snow obscure those lingering, negative memories and leave only the good ones? Could it bring back my little-girl memories of making snow ice cream with my mom in our kitchen in Tennessee? Could it remind my husband of coming into his Colorado home, his mittens frozen from building snowmen, to his mom's steaming hot cocoa with marshmallows? Could it leave us with memories of my mom arriving at our snowy airport in her smart tweed suit, or of his mom coming up the snowy walk for Thanksgiving dinner in her red coat, a bowl of homemade cranberry sauce in hand?

I knew I was expecting too much of the first snow that year, but it did come, and it did bring beauty and healing to our souls. Many snows have come and gone since then, and the grief is less with each passing year. If you have yet to go through the pain of losing your parent, or if your grief feels fresh and raw, believe your burden will lighten with time, because it will.

Ultimately, we must all let go. Let go of the regrets. Let go of the what-ifs. Let go of the if-onlys. And in time, let go of the grief.

I can't think of a better way to end this chapter, and this book, than to tell you about another beautiful letting-go experience that the Lord granted me.

I told the assisted living community where I volunteer that I couldn't come in for three months because of my deadline for this book. Yet I woke up the next Wednesday, my usual day to go, with no peace about my decision. I prayed for guidance. The devotion I read that morning centered on "serving in unnoticed places." Was that my answer? I began bargaining with the Lord: *But they aren't expecting me. But I didn't make cookies for today.* Still, I knew that the Holy Spirit was telling me to go, so I showered and went. Since they weren't planning to have class, I decided I would just visit some residents, particularly Sara, who was one of my favorites.

When I entered Sara's room, she was lying in her bed very still with the covers pulled up to her chin. Moving closer, I could see she had passed away. In the dead of winter, the air conditioning had been turned up full force. No one else was in the room, but I realized everyone there knew she was gone; they were just waiting for the funeral home to come pick her up.

I kissed Sara on the forehead and praised God for her life, and for sending me to say good-bye that day because He knew how devastated I would be if I hadn't had the chance to do so. I'll always remember the peaceful look and hint of a smile on Sara's face.

One day in class, she had asked me to explain the difference between cherubim and seraphim, so I looked it up. She laughed out loud when I told her that seraphim had three pairs of wings! All I could think as I looked down at her was, "Oh, Sara. You are seeing the seraphim now and smiling at them."

God is so good. No matter what, God is good. Trust that He will guide you to the end of your journey with your aging parent. Once the final letting go occurs, live in peace, knowing you did the best you could with the information you had. You took your parent's hand again. You honored. You cared. You loved.

Notes

Chapter 1

1. Claire Berman, *Caring for Yourself While Caring for Your Aging Parents* (New York: Henry Holt, 2005), 161–62.
2. John Haaga, "Just How Many Baby Boomers Are There?" Population Reference Bureau, December 2002, http://www.prb.org/Publications /Articles/2002/JustHowManyBabyBoomersAreThere.
3. "Aging Statistics," Administration on Aging, accessed January 5, 2012, http://www.aoa.gov/Aging_Statistics.
4. Beth Roalstad (executive director, Innovations in Aging), in an interview with the author, March 11, 2014.
5. Jane Gross, *A Bittersweet Season: Caring for Our Aging Parents—and Ourselves* (New York: Alfred A. Knopf, 2011), 231.
6. Ibid.
7. Virginia Wells, "Memories of Mom," *Ladies Home Journal*, August 1999,160. First published in *The Miami Herald*.
8. Henry T. Blackaby and Claude V. King, *Experiencing God* (Nashville: LifeWay, 1990), 127.
9. *Katie*, ABC, October 19, 2012.

Chapter 2

1. The Associated Press, "Hitler's Food Taster Tells of His Paranoia," *Colorado Springs Gazette*, Sunday, May 5, 2013, A15.

2. Emma Johnson, "5 Tough Parental Talks," *RealSimple*, March 2013, 115–18.

3. Ibid.

4. Dr. Sara Qualls in an interview with the author, March 19, 2014.

Chapter 3

1. Carol O'Dell, "What You Can Expect from a Great Assisted Living Community," Caring.com, accessed January 30, 2013, http://www .caring.com/articles/top-assisted-living-trends.

2. Paula Span, "When the Neighborhood Is the Retirement Village," *New York Times: The New Old Age* blog, September 25, 2009, http:// newoldage.blogs.nytimes.com/?s=When+the+Neighborhood+is+ the+Retirement+Village.

3. Ibid.

4. Sarah L. Delany and A. Elizabeth Delany with Amy Hill Hearth, *Having Our Say* (New York: Dell, 1993), 7–8.

5. "Multigenerational Households Are Increasing," AARP Public Policy Institute Fact Sheet, April 2011, http://blog.aarp.org/2011 /05/01/recession-increases-multigenerational-homes.

6. Kelly Greene, "New Retirement Resorts," *Wall Street Journal*, March 17–18, 2012, B10.

Chapter 5

1. Claire Berman, *Caring for Yourself While Caring for Your Aging Parents* (New York: Henry Holt, 2005), 96.

2. Jane Gross, *A Bittersweet Season: Caring for Our Aging Parents—and Ourselves* (New York: Alfred A. Knopf, 2011), 229.

3. *How to Help an Older Driver* (Washington, DC: AAA Foundation for Traffic Safety, 2002), http://seniordriving.aaa.com/sites/default /files/AAA-Foundation-Helping-Older-Driver.pdf.

4. Gross, *Bittersweet Season*, 230.

5. "Driver Still Cruising at 105," *Colorado Springs Gazette*, Thursday, June 6, 2013, A2.

6. *We Need to Talk . . . Family Conversations with Older Drivers* (Hartford, CT: The Hartford Center for Mature Market Excellence, 2013), http://www.thehartford.com/sites/thehartford/files/we-need -to-talk-2012.pdf.

7. Carol Bradley Bursack, "Talk," *Health Guide Saturday*, January 12, 2013.

8. Sally Abrahms, "Need a Ride?" *AARP Bulletin*, May 2013, 29.

Chapter 6

1. Joan Chittister, *The Gift of Years* (Katonah, NY: United Tribes Media, 2008), 81.

2. Ibid., 82.

3. Kathleen Fischer, *Winter Grace* (Nashville: Upper Room Books, 1998), 95.

4. Rachelle Zukerman, *Eldercare for Dummies* (Hoboken, NJ: Wiley Publishing, 2003), 270.

5. *Sisters Are Like Cookies and Milk* (Colorado Springs: Product Concept Mfg, 2011), 5, 7.

6. Missy Buchanan, *Living with Purpose in a Worn-out Body* (Nashville: Upper Room Books, 2008), 25.

7. Erin Prater, "Carson Babies Get Tender Care," *Colorado Springs Gazette*, November 3, 2013, F3.

8. Ibid.

9. Goodreads, quote from A. A. Milne, accessed January 15, 2015, https://www.goodreads.com/quotes/3026-if-you-live-to-be-a -hundred-i-want-to.

Chapter 7

1. The Associated Press, "Crossword Queen Marks 100 Years," *Colorado Springs Gazette*, January 14, 2014, A10.

2. Amanda Enayati, "The Aging Brain: Why Getting Older Just Might Be Awesome," CNN, June 19, 2012, http://www.cnn .com/2012/06/19/health/enayati-aging-brain-innovation/.

3. Robert Lee Hotz, "Brain Shrinkage: It's Only Human," *Wall Street Journal*, July 26, 2011, http://www.wsj.com/articles/SB100014240531 11903999904576468224286877908.

4. Mary Ann Kluge, PhD, "Physiology of Aging" (lecture presented at UCCS Professional Advancement Certificate in Gerontology program, September 27, 2011).

5. Enayati, "The Aging Brain."

6. "Signs of Dementia and How You Can Help Those You Love," December 12, 2011, https://www.humana.com/learning-center /health-and-wellbeing/mental-health/dementia.

7. Christine Wicker, "Unlocking the Silent Prison," *Parade Magazine*, November 21, 2010, 18.

8. *Desk Reference to the Diagnostic Criteria from DSM-5* (Washington, DC: American Psychiatric Association, 2013), 94.

9. Daniel L. Segal, PhD, "Understanding and Preventing Suicide Among Older Adults" (lecture presented at UCCS Professional Advancement Certificate in Gerontology program, September 13, 2011).

Chapter 8

1. "MIT Suit Makes Its Wearer Feel Old," *Los Angeles Times* as printed in *Colorado Springs Gazette*, January 4, 2012, A13.

2. "Life Expectancy," Social Security Administration, accessed January 15, 2015, www.socialsecurity.gov/planners/lifeexpectancy.htm.

3. Gail Sheehy, *New Passages* (New York: Random House, 1995), 408.

4. Charles R. Swindoll, *Strengthening Your Grip* (Waco: Word, 1982), 134.

5. Stephanie E. Cho, PharmD, Clinical Pharmacy Specialist, "Medicine and the Elderly" (lecture presented at UCCS Professional Advancement Certificate in Gerontology program, February 22, 2011).

6. Peter Jaret, "Older Adults: 9 Nutrients You May Be Missing,"

accessed February 2, 2014, http://www.webmd.com/healthy-aging
/nutrition-world-2/missing-nutrients.

7. Edith Wharton, *A Backward Glance*, "Thoughts," *Real Simple*,
September 2007, 10.

Chapter 9

1. R. Scott Rappold, "Last Run," *Colorado Springs Gazette*, Tuesday,
May 14, 2013.

2. Rebecca Ruiz, "Senior Citizen Cheerleading Squad Shows Spirit Is
Ageless," *The Today Show*, January 4, 2014, http://www.today.com
/news/senior-citizen-cheerleading-squad-shows-spirit-ageless
-2D11850693.

3. Velma Wallis, *Two Old Women* (New York: HarperCollins, 2004),
27.

4. Ibid., 28.

5. Jane Marie Thibault, *10 Gospel Promises for Later Life* (Nashville:
Upper Room Books, 2004), 99.

6. Charles R. Swindoll, Twitter.com, October 15, 2012.

7. "Quartet," directed by Dustin Hoffman, ©BBC Films, The
Weinstein Company, 2013.

8. "100 and Still Growing," *20/20*, ABC News, Transcript #1249, 12.

9. Brendan Moore, "Since End of U.S. Recession, More Seniors in
Workforce," October 17, 2013, http://www.gallup.com/poll/165470
/end-recession-seniors-workforce.aspx.

10. Kiri Tannenbaum, "McDonald's Celebrates Employee's 100th
Birthday," *Delish*, February 10, 2014, http://www.delish.com/food
/recalls-reviews/massachusetts-mcdonalds-employee-celebrates
-100th-birthday.

11. "Moving On," *AARP Bulletin*, November 2012, 8.

12. Virginia Campbell, interview on July 30, 2014.

13. Jane Gross, *A Bittersweet Season: Caring for Our Aging Parents—and
Ourselves* (New York: Alfred A. Knopf, 2011), 186.

14. Sally Abrahms, "The Power of Music," *AARP Bulletin*, March 2013, 10.

15. Beverly Morrone Haller, "Tell Us About a Time When You Jumped to the Wrong Conclusion," *Washington Post*, July 26, 2012, http://www.washingtonpost.com/lifestyle/magazine/editors-query-tell-us-about-a-time-when-you-jumped-to-the-wrong-conclusion/2012/07/26/gJQAaEIKeX_story.html.

16. Ann Hood, "The Girls," *Parade Magazine*, March 3, 2013, 14.

17. Sue Halpern, "Cold Nose, Warm Heart," *Parade Magazine*, May 5, 2013, 16.

18. Sally Abrahms, "A Comfort-and-Joy Approach," *AARP Bulletin*, July–August 2012, 14.

19. Cynthia Hubert, "Program Lets Seniors Keep Pets, Ensures They Get Care as Well," McClatchy Newspapers, as printed in *Colorado Springs Gazette*, March 5, 2013, D3.

20. Marilyn Doenges, RN, MA, CS, "Sexuality and Aging" (lecture presented at UCCS Professional Advancement Certificate in Gerontology program, September 6, 2011).

Chapter 10

1. Missy Buchanan, "A Note from the Heart," accessed January 15, 2015, http://www.missybuchanan.com/about/1-from-missy.

2. Eugene Peterson, *Answering God* (New York: HarperCollins, 1989), 92.

3. David Yonke, *The Blade*, April 28, 2012, www.toledoblade.com/Religion/2012/04/28/Study-finds-faith-key-to-aging-positively.

4. "Holy, Holy, Holy," lyrics by Reginald Heber. Public Domain.

5. "100 and Still Growing," *20/20*, ABC News, Transcript #1249, 13.

6. John W. James and Russell Friedman, *The Grief Recovery Handbook* (New York: HarperCollins e-books, 2009), 12–13.

7. Ron Ritchie, "Free at Last! Newsletter," Menlo Park, CA, February 2014.

Chapter 11

1. Statistics are from the National Alliance for Caregiving. Figures are current as of this writing. For further detailed statistics and updates, visit www.caregiving.org.

2. "A Focused Look at Those Caring for Someone Age 50 or Older," *Caregiving in the US*, 2009, National Alliance for Caregiving and AARP. Study funded by MetLife Foundation, http://www.care giving.org/data/FINALRegularExSum50plus.pdf.

3. Jane Gross, *A Bittersweet Season: Caring for Our Aging Parents—and Ourselves* (New York: Alfred A. Knopf, 2011), 174.

4. Missy Buchanan, "Aging Well: Eldercare Mediation Can Help Stressed-out Families," *The United Methodist Reporter*, December 12, 2012, http://unitedmethodistreporter.com/2012/12/12/ aging-well-eldercare-mediation-can-help-stressed-out-families/.

5. Ibid.

6. Elizabeth Pope, "Coming Together to Make Aging a Little Easier," *New York Times*, September 15, 2011, http://www.nytimes.com/2011 /09/16/business/retirementspecial/caring-collaborative-members -look-out-for-each-other.html?_r=0.

7. Dr. Nancy L. Snyderman, "My Life as a Caregiver," *AARP The Magazine*, October–November 2013.

8. Alicia Chang, "For Increasingly Many, It's Caregiving Times 2," *Colorado Springs Gazette*, January 1, 2012, A1, A4.

9. "When Siblings Step Up," *Wall Street Journal*, March 27–28, 2010, R4.

10. Ibid.

11. Amy Goyer, "A Crisis Around Every Corner," *AARP Bulletin*, November 2013.

12. Ibid.

13. Jonathan Rauch, "The Quiet Crisis," *Reader's Digest*, September 2011, 164. First published in *The Atlantic*.

14. Ibid., 166.

15. Ibid.

16. Celia Watson Seupel, "Broken, Briefly," *New York Times: The New Old Age* blog, December 9, 2011, http://newoldage.blogs.nytimes .com/2011/12/09/broken-briefly/?_r=0.

17. Ibid.

18. Jo Horne, "A Caregiver's Bill of Rights," accessed December 8, 2014, http://www.caregiver.com/articles/caregiver/caregiver_bill_of_rights .htm.

Chapter 12

1. Claire Berman, *Caring for Yourself While Caring for Your Aging Parents* (New York: Henry Holt, 2005), 108.

2. Sid Kirchheimer, "Love Me, Send Money," *AARP Bulletin*, July–August 2012, 18.

3. Ibid.

4. Sen. Bill Nelson, "Greater Numbers, Greater Risks," *AARP Bulletin*, June 2013, 38.

5. Berman, *Caring for Yourself*, 113–14.

6. Mary Pipher, *Another Country: Navigating the Emotional Terrain of Our Elders* (New York: Penguin Putnam, 1999), 144.

Chapter 13

1. Herbert Brokering, *I Will to You: Leaving a Legacy for Those You Love* (Minneapolis: Augsburg, 2006), 9.

2. Ibid., 11.

3. Henri Nouwen, *The Essential Nouwen*, ed. Robert A. Jonas (Boston: Shambhala Publications, 2009), 146–47.

4. Charles R. Swindoll, "Creating a Legacy of Forgiveness: Cancel the Debt," Insight for Living Ministries, accessed February 25, 2014, http://www.insight.org/resources/articles/christian-living/cancel-the -debt.html.

5. Henri J. M. Nouwen and Walter J. Gaffney, *Aging* (New York: Doubleday, 1974), 17.

6. Marty Norman, *Generation G* (Nashville: Nelson, 2007), 177.

7. Pamela Miller, "Billy Graham Examines Value of Old Age, Hope of Heaven," *Star Tribune*, as printed in the *Colorado Springs Gazette*, Saturday, April 14, 2007, LIFE7.

Chapter 14

1. Paula Span, "How Do You Want It to End?" *New York Times: The New Old Age* blog, August 17, 2012, http://newoldage.blogs.nytimes.com/?s=How+Do+You+Want+It+to+End%3F.

2. Ibid.

3. Hank Dunn, *Hard Choices for Loving People* (Herndon, VA: A & A Publishers, 1994), 38.

4. Ibid., 39.

5. Ibid., 46.

6. Katy Butler, *Knocking on Heaven's Door* (New York: Scribner, 2013), 4–5.

7. Katy Butler, "A Full Life to the End," *Wall Street Journal*, September 7–8, 2013, C1.

8. Carol Bradley Bursack, "Humor Provides Armor Against Caregivers' Deepest Sorrows," *Health Guide Sunday*, October 7, 2012.

Recommended Resources

Books

Berman, Claire. *Caring for Yourself While Caring for Your Aging Parents.* New York: Henry Holt, 2005.

Brummett, Nancy Parker. *The Hope of Glory: A Devotional Guide for Older Adults.* Raleigh: Lighthouse Publishing of the Carolinas, 2014.

Buchanan, Missy. *Living with Purpose in a Worn-out Body: Spiritual Encouragement for Older Adults.* Nashville: Upper Room Books, 2008.

Butler, Katy. *Knocking on Heaven's Door: The Path to a Better Way of Death.* New York: Simon & Schuster, 2013.

Chittister, Joan. *The Gift of Years: Growing Older Gracefully.* Katonah, NY: United Tribes Media, 2008.

Gross, Jane. *A Bittersweet Season: Caring for Our Aging Parents—and Ourselves.* New York: Knopf, 2011.

Mace, Nancy L., and Peter V. Rabins. *The 36-Hour Day: A Family Guide to Caring for People Who Have Alzheimer Disease, Related Dementias, and Memory Loss.* 5th ed. Baltimore: Johns Hopkins Press, 2011.

Nouwen, Henri J. M., and Walter J. Gaffney. *Aging: The Fulfillment of Life.* New York: Doubleday, 1990.

Pipher, Mary, PhD. *Another Country: Navigating the Emotional Terrain of Our Elders.* New York: Penguin Putnam, 1999.

Zukerman, Rachelle, PhD. *Eldercare for Dummies.* Hoboken, NJ: Wiley Publishing, 2003.

Websites

A Place for Mom, http://www.aplaceformom.com

Administration on Aging, http://www.aoa.gov

Alzheimer's Association, http://www.alz.org

American Association of Retired Persons (AARP), http://www.aarp.org

American Geriatrics Society, http://www.americangeriatrics.org

American Society on Aging, http://www.asaging.org

Eldercare Locator, http://www.eldercare.gov

National Alliance for Caregiving, http://www.caregiving.org

National Association of Area Agencies on Aging, http://www.n4a.org

National Association of Senior Move Managers, http://www.nasmm.org

National Center for Assisted Living, http://www.ahcancal.org/ncal

National Institute on Aging, http://www.nia.nih.gov

Rosalynn Carter Institute for Caregiving, http://www.rosalynncarter.org

Home Healthcare

Home Instead Senior Care, http://www.homeinstead.com

InnoVage, http://www.MyInnovAge.org

Interim HealthCare, http://www.interimhealth care.com

Right at Home, http://www.rightathome.net

Visiting Angels Home Care, http://www.visitingangels.com

Blogs

Carol Bradley Bursack's *Minding Our Elders*
http://www.mindingoureldersblogs.com

Missy Buchanan's *Reflections on Aging Well*
http://www.missybu.wordpress.com

Nancy Parker Brummett's *Take My Hand Again*
    http://www.nancyparkerbrummett.com/take-my-hand-again
New York Times: *The New Old Age*
    http://www.newoldage.blogs.nytimes.com

About the Author

Author and freelance writer Nancy Parker Brummett gained a heart for older adults as a child because her grandmother lived with her family, and she has enjoyed close friendships with many older adults over the years. She journeyed with her mother and mother-in-law through their adventures in aging, and her academic interest in aging led her to receive the Professional Advancement Certificate in Gerontology from the University of Colorado at Colorado Springs.

Nancy's other books include *Simply the Savior*, *It Takes a Home*, *The Journey of Elisa*, *Reconcilable Differences*, and *The Hope of Glory*, a devotional guide for older adults. Nancy is now focusing her writing and speaking ministries on her passion for older adults and those who care for them. She and her husband, Jim, live in Colorado Springs. They have four grown children, twelve grandchildren, and two cats in their blended family. To learn more about Nancy's life and work, or to subscribe to her blog on aging issues, *Take My Hand Again*, visit her website at www.nancyparkerbrummett.com.